THE
RIDING INSTRUCTOR'S
HANDBOOK

THE
RIDING
INSTRUCTOR'S
HANDBOOK

Monty Mortimer

DAVID & CHARLES
Newton Abbot   London

(*opposite title page*) Nick Skelton of Great Britain on Everest Lastic jumping in Geneva (*Findlay Davidson*)

British Library Cataloguing in Publication Data

Mortimer, Monty
   The riding instructor's handbook.
   1. Horsemanship
   I. Title
   798′.23′07   SF309

   ISBN 0–7153–8102–4

First published 1981
Second impression 1983

Typeset by Typesetters (Birmingham) Limited,
and printed in Great Britain
by Biddles Limited, Guildford, Surrey
for David & Charles (Publishers) Limited
Brunel House   Newton Abbot   Devon

Contents

Foreword

The survival of all species is dependent on the instinct to follow the example and teaching of others. Fortunately for mankind the desire to share one's knowledge and ability is almost universal. It is after all a form of immortality.

Books in their thousands are at hand to cater for this inborn need to acquire knowledge but, certainly in the equestrian world, it is rare if not unique to find one which specialises in *how* not *what* to teach.

Major Mortimer's book does this admirably. His clarity of thought and attention to detail are supported by a simple well written text and excellent illustrations. There is also a very refreshing lack of bias towards any particular method or school of thought.

But for me, its greatest value lies not in the written word but in the dedication and deep love of teaching which slowly becomes apparent between the lines. Without this, however great one's knowledge and riding ability, the 'gift' of teaching will never be bestowed.

SHEILA INDERWICK

Introduction

Having taught a wide range of subjects for some twenty-five years, it occurred to me that very little has been written on how to actually teach a particular skill or theory. I have therefore tried, in this short work, to suggest ways in which those of you who are so devoted to your subject that you wish to share it with others by teaching may achieve your aim with the greatest effect.

Many volumes have been written on the horse and how it should be ridden, and this book is not intended to be added to that list. Where I have strayed into the subject of equitation or horsemastership it is intended only to assist the riding instructor in teaching his subject.

The rider has been referred to throughout the book as 'he'. This is not due to any chauvinistic prejudice but to avoid the rather cumbersome, continual reference to 'he/she'.

The riding instructor is generally thought to be one who teaches people to ride horses. To do this he has to depend very largely on the goodwill of his staunch friend and assistant, the horse. Ideally we would have a pool of correctly trained horses on which we would train novice riders and a pool of expert riders who would train our young horses. This utopian situation is unlikely ever to be achieved.

It is however impossible to separate the training of the rider from the training of the horse. Except in the very early stages of teaching the novice rider, where a trained horse has to be used, the instructor will usually find himself teaching a novice rider on a novice horse. Under these circumstances, as the rider improves so the horse will follow, and it is with this situation in mind that this book has been written.

For many years we have benefited from the very high standard of riding instruction that was maintained in the world's major cavalry schools, but we are now sadly coming to the end of the very expert instructors trained by those schools. The responsibility for training riding instructors has now passed to civilian riding schools, and the various national bodies whose task is to guide and protect the interests of horses and riders. Their teaching principles are largely based on those of their military predecessors, as are those advocated in this book.

Many roads lead to Rome and it is stressed that the route suggested here is by no means the only one. It has been thoroughly tried and it works; it is therefore humbly offered for consideration by anyone who is setting out to teach this fascinating subject.

MONTY MORTIMER

1
The Qualities of a Good Instructor

'Those who can, do, and those who can't, teach.' Whilst this comment is often made by the cynic, it does not follow that an expert on any subject will necessarily be able to pass on his knowledge or skill to others. Many expert teachers are, however, failed or disappointed competitors, who, although in no way lacking in enthusiasm, have through lack of funds, opportunity or ability, failed to make the grade in their chosen sport. Whilst to be a National or Olympic Champion or an International competitor is sure to enhance the reputation of an instructor, these qualities do not necessarily make a good teacher. There are many other qualities which contribute to making a successful instructor.

Knowledge of his subject
His knowledge must be sound and in considerable depth and detail. The complete instructor will have studied his subject and discussed it minutely with his fellow teachers. To have complete confidence in the doctrine that he is trying to put across to his pupils he must have dissected it, taken it apart and questioned it from every angle. Only in this way will he remove that which is irrelevant, untrue or just 'an old wives' tale', so many examples of which flourish in the riding world.

His teaching will be constantly under scrutiny from his pupils and often from his fellows; so whilst he should never be over-dogmatic or unbending the ability to defend his principles from a firm base of study and detailed consideration of the facts is vital.

It is important that the instructor has a wide and detailed knowledge of schools of teaching other than his own. Only with this knowledge will he be able to justify his theories in relation to the theories of others. If he is vigorously opposed to any movement or exercise he should know quite clearly why he objects to it and equally clearly why it is practised so widely and successfully by other trainers. Only with this depth of prepared and analysed knowledge will he be able to teach with confidence.

Confidence

A riding instructor's pupils will often be nervous; his confidence will help to overcome their nervousness. Confidence will come with experience but will depend upon his own ability to teach; his thorough knowledge of his subject and how to teach it; his own expertise as a performer in any required skills and the preparation and planning of his lesson.

Enthusiasm

The good instructor must 'sell' his subject. His attitude should be rather like a salesman earning his pay on commission. Enthusiasm is infectious, and the instructor's enthusiasm will soon be imparted to his class.

Many instructors will teach several classes each day, and it is reasonable to assume that their enthusiasm will wane towards the end of the day. It must be remembered though that each new class of pupils starts fresh and expects a cheerful, enthusiastic teacher. They may not know, or even care, that he is taking his fifth or sixth class that day. They are, after all, paying for their instruction and deserve and expect enthusiastic teaching.

Manner

The instructor's manner must be bold and confident. His appearance is of vital importance. It is only good manners to appear before the class properly dressed in riding clothes. The pupils should notice the shine on the instructor's boots and that his breeches, jacket, collar and tie are clean and well fitting. Whilst it is usual for an instructor to wear a hat, men need not necessarily teach in a hard hat but lady instructors usually do. The instructor should always wear gloves and carry a riding whip. A slovenly appearance usually leads to slack instruction and a poor class reaction.

Instructors are sometimes seen smoking, leaning against the kicking boards of the school or even drinking their coffee whilst teaching. These are all aspects of an unacceptable manner in the riding instructor.

The use of the voice is an aspect of teaching which is often neglected; it must be clear and loud enough to be heard by all the pupils in the class, but this is difficult for some people to achieve without shouting. Lady instructors sometimes find this more difficult to achieve than men, but it can be done. It is not so offensive to the ear to hear a man shout an instruction but it always grates to hear a lady shouting. There are however many very successful lady instructors who manage to make themselves heard in a clear and charming way.

The tone of the voice is important and whilst to instruct in monotones can sound very boring, too much of a 'singsong' voice can be distracting. The instructor must strive to find the happy medium of speed, pitch and tone. It is often very revealing to record one's own voice on tape whilst teaching, and many instructors would learn a lot about the way in which they teach on playing the tape back.

Riding training is usually carried out at a distance and it is often difficult for an instructor to make himself heard and understood. Clear diction and well chosen words will help. Whilst instructions must be given in a commanding way they must not sound like parade ground drill orders. The instructor's tone of voice must be encouraging, and must never show any sign of exasperation or loss of temper.

Above all an instructor must avoid a nagging or complaining tone of voice.

Patience and understanding
To teach any subject the instructor requires endless patience, and the ability to understand his pupils' problems. Most instructors will be passionately keen on their subject. When teaching riding the instructor must be able to assess his pupils' ambitions and limitations, both natural and self-imposed. Not every rider will have Olympic aspirations but will be happy to hack out safely on a trained horse. The understanding instructor will appreciate this and modify his teaching accordingly. Similarly he will be able to cater for the competition rider who is striving for ever greater goals.

The good instructor will quickly identify the nervous rider or the rider whose conformation prevents him from achieving the correct riding position or application of the aids. It is sometimes difficult to understand how one student can find rising trot so difficult, or how another finds mounting such a task, but it is the duty of the good instructor to put himself in the position of these riders. and so, taking their background and physical make-up into consideration, find the answer. This sort of challenge is what makes the teaching of any subject so fascinating and rewarding.

A sense of humour
There are very few professions in which a sense of humour is not an immense asset. People ride horses mainly for enjoyment and this can be increased by an instructor who has a good sense of humour. In fact it is safe to say that a riding instructor who does not have a fairly highly developed sense of fun is destined to a dull and frustrating career.

However care must be taken not to be facetious or sarcastic, and every student of riding must learn to tolerate mild leg-pulling from his instructor. The age and personality of an instructor will dictate how far this can be carried. A Sergeant Major riding instructor was once heard to say to a class of young officers, 'It's all a question of mind over matter, gentlemen — I don't mind and you don't matter.' It was an amusing remark under the circumstances, but would not sound well coming from an eighteen-year-old Assistant Instructor taking a class of novice adults.

The instructor-student relationship
The instructor must set the standards that will determine the relationship that is to exist between him and his pupils. He should learn each pupil's background, and be quick to appreciate each individual's physical and mental limitations and difficulties.

Apart from the entirely aesthetic importance of correct riding dress, it is difficult to make progress in riding without the correct clothing and the instructor must set the necessary standard. By his own good example, he will establish a standard in his pupils which will be both of help to them and a credit to him. It is unreasonable to expect an absolute beginner

The instructor-student relationship at the Cadre Noir, Saumur, France (*Author*)

to appear for his first lesson correctly dressed for riding. However he must wear, apart from his normal clothes, sensible shoes, gloves and a hard hat.

Whilst it is of great importance that there is communication in both directions between instructor and pupil, progress is best made if the instructor gives commands and the pupil diligently and enthusiastically tries to carry them out. Throughout the lesson, whether it be a class or individual lesson, the instructor must make a break where he gives his pupils the opportunity to ask questions. Where no questions are forthcoming, as is so often the case, he must stimulate useful discussion by putting relevant questions to the class.

The instructor must establish his own reputation and credibility by teaching with sincerity and sympathy; he must be demanding and yet understanding, and above all he must realise his pupils' ambitions and limitations. For some students, riding is just for fun and exercise; these pupils must be catered for as they contribute an important part to the riding school economy and often; under the right instructor, change their attitude and aspire to become serious horsemen. For the serious student of classical equitation no demand from the instructor, within the student's immediate limitations at that time, is too great. For this student absolute perfection must be considered as only just good enough.

2
Teaching the Beginner

The rider's first few lessons are usually designed to overcome a combination of the following factors: fear, ignorance, lack of physical fitness and general lack of horse understanding. Fear is best overcome by the provision of the correct horse. He must of course be placid, quiet and used to being ridden by novices. He must stand still whilst being mounted and dismounted but must also respond to the rider's aids and trainer's voice. Once a beginner rider has established a rapport with, and is confident in, a particular horse, it is very much to his advantage to be allowed to ride that horse at each lesson until his confidence is such that he can go on to greater things.

The quiet, confident and friendly attitude of the instructor will help to allay the rider's fears, as will a quiet training area or riding school free from distractions or any sort of alarm. It is a disaster for any beginner rider to fall off his horse or be run away with. Should either of these situations arise, the instructor must question his training methods closely in an attempt to discover where the fault lies. It is very often due to an unsuitable horse being provided or the rider being asked to perform an exercise for which he is not ready. One thing is certain, however, that a mishap of this sort can only be a setback in the training of a novice rider.

Fear is not always overcome by improving the pupil's familiarity with the horse, but tasks such as saddling up, mucking out and grooming will improve the student's confidence in the horse in general which will, hopefully, be reflected in his riding.

Ignorance can be a problem where beginner riders come from the city centre or suburbs, as they are currently doing in increasing numbers, and probably have no knowledge of large animals. It is sometimes difficult for those of us who have spent many years with horses to understand how the

Berteland de Nemethy, one of the world's most successful trainers, at the indoor school at the British Equestrian Centre, Kenilworth, Warwickshire (*Findlay Davidson*)

uninitiated can have such a lack of understanding. The beginner rider so often compares horse riding with driving his car and he cannot understand why the accelerator, brakes and steering on his horse do not work as reliably as they do in his car. It probably does not occur to him how simple careless actions around the horse can have disastrous results. Leaving the stable door open, taking the reins over the horse's head and letting them drop on the ground and landing in the saddle with a thump when mounting are typical small points of basic instruction which the experienced rider would take for granted, but which no instructor can assume will be taken for granted by a beginner rider. For the sake of safety and progress, basic elements of simple horse management must go hand in glove with riding training.

Riding, in its simplest form, is physically demanding and to the beginner, who may be tense and making unnecessary physical effort as a consequence, it is even more strenuous. People, as a rule, tend not to stand up straight, sit up straight, or carry themselves with good deportment. As soon as they start to ride, however, we ask them to sit in an upright position, with their bodies in a correct shape. Further, we ask them to sit astride the horse with their legs apart making the joint where the top of the femur fits into the pelvis open sideways and forwards, and to maintain that position throughout their ride. This puts a strain on the muscles which control these joints in a way which the student has probably never experienced before. We then ask the student to carry the toe a little higher than the heel, which may cause stiffening of the calf muscles. The average beginner will not be fit enough to carry out the instructor's demands with regard to position for some time. The observant instructor will be conscious of this and will take the rider's fitness into consideration when giving his instruction. Together with this must be considered the shape of the rider; some people have very round shoulders or short fat thighs, or are very tall or too fat, or have a combination of physical peculiarities which prevent them from attaining a classically perfect position. It is the duty of the riding instructor to achieve the best possible results that he can within the individual limitations of each rider.

An excellent outdoor training area with an all-weather wood fibre surface and safe fencing (*Author*)

The First Lesson

The best way to start off a beginner rider is on the lunge. In this way the horse is under the complete control of the instructor and the student can concentrate on the development of his seat and position without being concerned with the control of the horse in any way. If the first lesson is taken as a class lesson with the pupils riding free, so many assistants are needed that individual private lessons would have been easier to run in the first place. Half an hour on the lunge will result in much more real progress being made than in a one hour class lesson of first time riders.

For the first lesson the horse should be dressed in a suitable saddle (not forward cut), neck strap, snaffle bridle, side reins, lunge cavesson, lunge rein and brushing boots. Having checked that the rider is suitably dressed, from a point of safety only, the instructor should show him how to lead the horse out of the loose box and into the school. It is a good start for the student to do this on his first day.

The reins safely secured before lungeing. Note the snug fit of the lunge cavesson (*John W. Benson*)

The rules of the riding school must be taught and observed from the very beginning. These include knocking on the riding school door and asking for permission to enter, or whatever the local rule may be, and forming up correctly on the centre line to mount under control.

Correct mounting and dismounting should be taught at this stage; it is of considerable importance to the rider, the horse and the saddle that this is done correctly. The competent instructor will never allow it to be carried out incorrectly. Mounting and dismounting on both the near and off sides must be taught but the offside will come later, as will mounting without stirrups. The instructor should demonstrate the correct way to mount and dismount, explaining what he is doing as he goes through the actions.

The practice of dismounting by throwing the right leg over the horse's withers and dropping to the ground should be forbidden. It is potentially dangerous, tends to be very infectious and is quickly picked up and copied by young riders. If this practice is allowed to become a habit, and a horse does shy or take fright once the rider has dropped his reins and has got his right leg part way over the horse's withers, the result can be very dangerous.

Skills are best taught by:

EXPLANATION

DEMONSTRATION

APPLICATION

Here the instructor explains and demonstrates at the same time. On occasions it will be found to be advantageous to demonstrate, then explain, and then allow the student to apply the teaching.

Once the rider is in the saddle he must be taught, quickly, how to hold both reins in one hand whilst he uses the other hand to adjust his stirrup leather, and then to change the reins to the opposite hand whilst he adjusts the other stirrup leather. A beginner rider must never be allowed to drop the reins whilst he uses both hands to adjust one stirrup leather or to take his foot out of the stirrup iron. This is often seen but it is incorrect, idle and dangerous. If adjusting the stirrup leathers is taught correctly from the start it will not be long before the rider can adjust them quickly at halt or as he moves along without looking down, which is so necessary to the practical horseman. This simple task is often made difficult by poorly kept saddles and stirrup leathers, leathers that are stiff or too thick for the stirrup bars, worn out buckles, or pairs of leathers with holes that do not match. A combination of these factors can make stirrup adjustment difficult even for the most experienced rider.

When the stirrups have been adjusted correctly and the rider understands which way to put his foot into the stirrup iron without twisting the leather, he must be shown how to hold the reins even though he will not hold them at first whilst he is being lunged. Then, whilst still at halt, the instructor must go quickly through the correct position in the saddle. At this stage it is sufficient to get the rider to sit in the lowest part of the saddle and as straight as possible, and he should be shown which part of his foot should be on the stirrup iron.

Remember the student has come to *ride*, and as by now half the lesson time will have passed he will be beginning to wonder

The correct seat at halt (*John W. Benson*)

how much of riding is administration, protocol and preparation and how much is actual riding. The good instructor will know the importance of correct preparation, but he will also know how important it is to get on with the job of riding as soon as possible. At this stage the reins should be taken from the rider, twisted under the horse's gullet and secured by the throat lash.

The student is asked to hold the pommel of the saddle by looping one or two fingers of each hand underneath it. The way in which the pommel is held is important as, if it is held incorrectly, the rider may push himself up and out of the saddle and not pull himself down and into the saddle which was the original intention.

The horse and rider are now ready to be moved off into walk by the instructor, and it is important that the pupil is told what is going to happen. The instructor must explain that he is in control of the horse completely and that the rider need do nothing but relax and try to carry out his instructions.

Once the horse is on the lunge circle in walk the instructor can start to improve the rider's position. As so much time and effort is spent on achieving a correct riding position the pupil should be told why it is so important, and this is as good a stage as any to do this. It will give the student 'the reason why' (an important aspect of all training) and it will give him something to think about and help to relax him during these first few circles at walk. It should be explained to him at this stage that there are three main reasons for achieving a correct position.

The first is that the horse was not designed to carry a rider on his back. If we want the horse to perform well for us, therefore, we should make the load that we ask him to carry as well balanced as possible. This will make the task of both horse and rider very much easier. It is often helpful to make an analogy to stress a point. Here we might make the comparison of carrying 15lb of shopping home in two shopping baskets; it is much easier to carry if you have 7.5lb in each basket, thus balancing the load, than if you have 5lb in one basket and 10lb in the other.

The second reason for sitting in the correct position is that the rider must be able to apply the aids with his legs, his seat and his hands quickly and effectively. This can best be achieved from sitting correctly in the saddle.

The third reason is that the rider should try to look as elegant as possible. The combination of horse and rider must be pleasing to the spectator's eye, and the classical correctness of the rider's position will play a major part in achieving this. At this stage in the rider's training the importance of suppleness and controlled relaxation must be mentioned. Tenseness and stiffness are equally disastrous in both horse and rider, and will be the result of apprehension and lack of confidence at this stage. It is therefore the instructor's first task to put the pupil at ease and to improve his confidence, and this is best done by getting the pupil to carry out a series of exercises. When the instructor sees that the moment is right he can ask the rider to let go of the saddle with his inside hand only, and rest that hand on his thigh. He can then ask the rider to stretch that arm out level with his shoulder, and to make large circles slowly backwards with the arm whilst keeping his shoulders square to the front. After five or six circles he should be told to rest, hold the pommel with both hands again, and then repeat the exercise with the outside arm. By now it will be time to change the rein, as to work equally on both reins is of vital importance if the horse and rider are to progress in an even and balanced fashion.

Provided that this training has proceeded according to plan the next exercise can be attempted. Here the rider is asked to let go of the saddle with both hands, and to rest them on his thighs. When he is seen to be confident and balanced, the instructor can ask him to stretch both arms out level with his shoulders and to make large circles slowly backwards with both arms. Care must be taken to see that he does not grip up with his knees, calves or heels when he lets go with both hands. It is a natural reaction, but is clearly wrong. Part of the value of these exercises is that the rider should be able to isolate and exercise one part of the body whilst leaving the rest of the body still and supple, and in the correct position.

There are many exercises that the imaginative instructor can introduce into this first lesson, some of which are particularly useful in correcting a particular fault. For example, where a rider persistently has trouble with the right

(*opposite*) The correct riding position at halt from the rear (*By courtesy of the British Horse Society*)

Fig 1 Exercises to improve suppleness on the lunge, moving one and then both arms in a full circle

shoulder coming in front of the left shoulder, a short session of work on the lunge can be beneficial, during which he should hold the pommel of the saddle with his left hand and the cantle with his right hand.

Almost any exercise which will improve the rider's confidence, suppleness, agility and understanding is acceptable, provided that it is safe and will not create a problem later on in the rider's training (Fig. 1). If possible this first lesson should be completed with a circuit or two on each rein in sitting trot. It will give the rider an incentive, it will give him 'a look forward' to the next lesson and it will finish the lesson with a sense of real achievement.

The rider must be given the opportunity to ask questions before he dismounts, and must be made to dismount properly, run up the stirrup irons, loosen the girth and turn the horse in correctly. This is an extremely important aspect of all riding training.

In the interests of safety the side reins should only be fitted to the bit whilst the horse is working. They should be detached from the bit and secured to the 'D' rings on the saddle whilst the horse is being led to and from the stable, and when the rider is mounting and dismounting.

The actual lungeing of the horse is dealt with in Chapter 4.

The Second Lesson

In this lesson the rider continues on the lunge. Once again he collects his horse from the stable and, under supervision, leads it into the school where he checks the girth and adjusts the stirrups. Most beginners of average physical fitness will be able to mount satisfactorily on their own. There may be cases where the overweight, more elderly or less agile pupil will need a mounting block or a leg up. Both these methods of mounting should be taught, if only in the interest of the horse's comfort.

Work on the lunge at this stage of training is vital, but it must be kept interesting and the pupil must not be allowed to feel that because he is not riding free he is not making progress. It would benefit the beginner rider greatly to keep him on the lunge for much longer than we usually do, and in some famous riding schools the trainee rider is kept on the lunge for some years before being allowed to ride free.

However desirable this may be, some practical considerations do have to be taken into account.

Firstly, most trainee riders want to get on and ride on their own and there is a chance that they will lose interest if they are kept on the lunge for too long; secondly, it must be more expensive for them to have private lunge lessons than to join a class; and thirdly, it is usually uneconomical from an instructor's point of view, as it is often not possible to charge a realistic fee for individual instruction.

This subject is raised here because it is from the second lesson onwards that the instructor must begin to ask himself 'When will this pupil be ready to join a novice class lesson?'

In this second lesson, work must start at walk again and the main points of the last lesson be revised. As soon as the exercises are mastered in walk and the rider is sitting in approximately the right position then work must start in sitting trot. As his confidence improves he can be asked to make the arm circling and trunk twisting exercise in sitting trot, and the instructor must remember to make regular and frequent changes of rein. Throughout this lesson the instructor must correct the rider's position, and should encourage him to sit deep in the lowest part of the saddle in a supple upright way. He must be told to try to blend the movement of his body into the movement of the horse's back, and it should be made clear to him that he should not make more movement with his body than the horse makes for him.

The astute instructor will recognise the time when he can ask his pupil to take away the stirrups, which may well occur during the second lunge lesson. Whilst it is emphasised that this work on the lunge is done to get the rider in the correct position and sitting in the bottom of the saddle, the safety and confidence of the pupil must be taken into consideration.

Where the use of stirrups on the lunge is concerned, there is a conflict of interests. It is clearly an advantage for the beginner to have the use of his stirrups to improve his safety and confidence, but it is a disadvantage if the rider learns to depend too often or too quickly on the stirrups for his security. A much deeper seat and a better feel for the movement of the horse will be built into the rider who is trained on the lunge without stirrups. However, common sense must prevail and where the pupil is clearly nervous or is insufficiently fit or agile he should be made to take his stirrups for the first few sessions. The instructor at this stage can watch for the opportunity to introduce his student to rising trot. There is no set stage, and the instructor should recognise when his student is ready. The rider who shows good co-ordination and is obviously comfortable and in harmony and balance with the lunge horse will sometimes make a few voluntary steps in rising trot without being asked to do so; this should be noticed by the instructor and encouraged. This is, however, not always the case, and the instructor must explain to his pupil what is required in rising trot. The pupil's attention should be drawn to a rider who is executing a good rising trot and the movement should be explained to him. He can then practise the movement a little at halt. This should not be overdone as it is difficult to do correctly, and the feeling is not quite the same as the up and down movement required at trot.

When practising rising trot on the lunge the circle must be a little bigger, up to about 5m and the horse must be sent on a little faster and with rather more impulsion. It is difficult for a beginner to pick up rising trot if the pace is too slow or the impulsion insufficient. Rhythm plays a very important part in rising trot and a good rhythm is more likely to be achieved if the speed of the trot is good and the impulsion sufficient.

To introduce the rider to rising trot whilst he is holding the pommel of the saddle is a mistake as it creates a rather cramped and stiff feeling. It is preferable if he can carry his hands as though he were holding the reins, but if he is unbalanced, he can rest his hands on his thighs. Holding the neck strap is a further alternative, but there is the danger here that he will learn to pull himself up by using the neck strap and this could lead to pulling himself up with the reins. The disadvantages of this need no explanation.

The diagonal on which he is rising at this stage is of no importance, as this can be taught later. If it is introduced here it may only complicate what to some pupils is already a difficult exercise in co-ordination.

Both rider and instructor will have made good progress if they have carried out some useful gymnastic exercises at walk and sitting trot, have started to establish a correct rider's position and have achieved a few circuits in rising trot by the end of the second lunge lesson.

Beginner riders come in all shapes and sizes. They will range from the unathletic, overweight person who may be teenaged, middle-aged or somewhere in between, to the fit, lithe, agile person who has played other games successfully and has good mind and muscle co-ordination.

The good instructor will quickly assess his pupil and know how much to ask from him. Some will thrive on being extended to their limits, others will have to be nursed very carefully, both physically and mentally, and there are many somewhere between these extremes. Half an hour is sufficient for the beginner's lunge lesson, and if he is made to work correctly this lesson can be very demanding physically. The horse too must be considered, as a half hour lunge lesson in which he will probably work for twenty minutes will be plenty for him.

Whilst all riders will want to progress, the instructor must take care not to rush these first vital lessons. It should be remembered that 'haste is the enemy of perfection'.

The Third Lesson

If normal, average progress has been achieved this should be the last of the beginner's lunge lessons. In the first two lessons we worked on establishing the correct basic position, and tried to build up the rider's confidence by giving him simple gymnastic exercises to do at halt, walk and sitting trot. Rising trot was then introduced.

In the third lesson the rider is taught how to hold the reins, and is made to ride holding them in walk and trot. Once this has been completed the instructor can explain the aids and how they are applied. At this stage he will be limited to the aids for the upward and downward transitions from halt through walk and trot and back down to halt. The aids to turn to the left and right can be explained here but cannot be practised until the pupil is off the lunge.

The aids can now be put into effect by the rider to coincide with the instructor's commands to the horse. As the rider's aids improve and become more effective, so the instructor can reduce his commands to the horse until the rider is controlling the horse with his own aids although still on the lunge.

This lesson can be concluded by removing the lunge cavesson and side reins and allowing the rider to ride loose in

A correct, natural position, without strain or tension (*Author*)

the school, practising progressive transitions from halt, through walk and trot and back down through walk to halt. As his confidence improves, the aids to turn and circle can be practised and the rider will be ready to join a suitable class for his next lesson.

A few general points on teaching the absolute beginner are appropriate here. The correct riding position is of fundamental importance and in the first lesson it was explained to the pupil why it is so important. When explaining to the pupil the correct way in which to sit, the choice of words and expressions that the instructor uses will have a direct effect for good or ill; he must therefore consider the words he uses very carefully. Most students will do their very best to carry out the instructor's commands, some to such an extent that they try too hard and this may have an adverse effect. The versatile instructor will use a variety of expressions to achieve the same end. To persuade the rider to hold the upper part of his body in the correct position the instructor can use a number of different phrases, such as 'Sit up straight', 'Square the shoulders', 'Shoulders back', 'Hollow the back', 'Close the shoulder blades', and many other expressions which will have a similar result. Some of these expressions, however, will have an adverse effect on some riders. To ask a rider to 'Square his shoulders' often results in him pulling his elbows behind his back and stiffening his neck and shoulders. Perhaps the best expression to use in order to achieve the correct shape of the upper body is to ask him to 'Lift up the chest and put it out' as this puts the upper part of the body into the required position without introducing any stiffness or tension.

There are many ways to ensure that the rider holds his head

The single rein correctly held (*Author*)

in a natural, controlled but relaxed position. One very good way to achieve this is to ask him to 'point his nose and his chin between the horse's ears and feel the back of his neck in the back of his collar'. He should be told that he can look down at his horse as much as he likes but he must learn to look down along his nose, out of the bottom of his eyes and without tipping his head down.

Explaining to the rider the correct way in which to hold the reins sometimes presents the instructor with a problem. It can be explained by likening the rein to a little bird held in the hand; if you hold it too tightly you will crush it and if you hold it too loosely it will fly away.

When describing how the arms should be carried it is very helpful to explain that there should be an imaginary straight line from the rider's elbow, through his little finger, to the bit. The top of the arm should be held close to the rider's side, not too closely but just allowing the inside of the sleeve to brush against the side of the jacket.

The use of an analogy is sometimes helpful. The way the rider's leg should hang around the horse's side has been likened to 'a wet dish cloth flopped over the side of the kitchen sink'. This is a particularly imaginative comparison and can obtain exactly the right result in some cases.

The choice of the right words or expressions can be as useful and helpful as the choice of the wrong words can be harmful and misleading.

3

The Class Lesson

Class lessons are useful as they provide an economical way of training a number of riders at the same time in a limited area. A good instructor will soon create an air of camaraderie in his class; a feeling that all his pupils have a common aim and that they are each confronted with similar problems.

To be successful, a class lesson should not contain more than eight pupils. A very experienced instructor may handle more, but the success of a larger class will depend on the degree of competence of the students and how capable they are of working on their own within the class. In any class, the more pupils there are the less individual instruction each person will be given.

To control this class effectively the instructor will require a riding school approximately 40m by 20m or a fenced-in, outdoor arena of similar dimensions. A slightly larger school has obvious advantages, but a class of eight can be trained

Fig 2 The riding school layout, showing the four circle points

A class of well mounted, neatly dressed riders ready for inspection before the lesson (*Author*)

satisfactorily by a competent instructor in an area this size. The schooling area must be marked out with reference points (Fig. 2), and these are essential for the instructor to be able to command the ride effectively.

A class ride should ideally consist of riders of an equal or at least a very similar standard. If the standard within the ride varies too greatly it can be frustrating for the more advanced riders. The class does, of necessity, have to progress at the pace of the slowest pupil; and whilst even the most advanced rider should be prepared to work on and revise the basic principles, the frustration which may be caused in these circumstances must be appreciated.

The choice of horses for a class ride requires careful consideration. To have one or two horses that are onward bound and one or two who get left behind can cause chaos in the class and can detract from its efficiency to a great extent. It is therefore important that both riders and horses are of a uniform standard as far as possible. For a successful class lesson the practical instructor will arrange to have a trained rider as leading file. This precaution will serve two major purposes: firstly, he will be able to set a sure, steady, even pace at walk, trot and canter, and secondly, he will be able to demonstrate to the class when required to do so.

The object of a class lesson is to involve as many riders as possible in maximum activity, simultaneously and under control. The class that is being considered here is a class of novices, and methods of teaching a class of more advanced riders will be considered later in this chapter.

Most class lessons are programmed for one hour, and if the whole hour is used constructively it is sufficient for both horse and rider. At the start of the lesson the instructor must introduce himself to the class. This should be done if it is the first time that he has taught the class, or if any individual person has just joined them. It is only good manners and creates a better class spirit if the individual members of the class are introduced to one another, and this applies particularly to new members joining the class.

It is important that the instructor finds out about the standard of training of his pupils before the start of the lesson. If he waits until the beginning of the lesson he will not be able to plan his work, which will result in an 'off the cuff' air in his teaching.

The instructor should be quick to learn the students' names. It is unacceptable to refer to a student by his number in the ride (except on some special occasions described later) or by the name of the horse. Remembering names is difficult for some instructors, particularly when they are teaching several classes every day and may see some of their students only once a week. It is however a skill which has to be developed and will certainly impress and even flatter some students if the instructor can achieve it, especially as it may even offend those whose names have been forgotten.

Each member of the class should collect his horse from the stable and, under supervision, lead it correctly into the riding school to form up on the centre line. They should stand in a straight line with a safe distance between each horse, the student standing correctly at the horse's head with the stirrups down and girth checked ready to mount. The instructor gives the word to mount, which he supervises carefully to see that it is carried out correctly by each member of the class. Once the class is mounted, each member should be inspected to see that the tack is fitted correctly and that the girths are adjusted. At this stage, if necessary, the class can be taught how to adjust the girth when mounted.

The instructor must insist that each rider sits correctly in the saddle right from the start of the lesson. As he inspects the pupils he has the opportunity to correct the way in which they are sitting. This will include ensuring that the rider has his foot in the correct side of the stirrup iron, a mistake so often made by the beginner when mounting.

Once all the preliminaries have been completed work can be started, as the ride should never be left standing still for too long. It is bad for horses to be kept standing still with riders on their backs and both horses and riders soon get cold. Sufficient rest periods must be provided throughout the lesson for both horse and rider but at the start of the lesson one should proceed with the actual riding as soon as possible; after all, that is what the riders have come to do.

The instructor must now give the command for the ride to move off. As they are on the centre line at rest, he may say, 'Take up your reins, correct the position — and walk march; on reaching the track left turn in single file.' There are several ways in which the commands can be given. The commands suggested throughout this book are recommended as being short, clear and precise. Each command must have a 'cautionary word of command' to warn and prepare the ride, followed by an 'executive word of command' on which the instruction is actually carried out.

The ride is now in walk on the left rein following a trained leading file who is setting a steady, even pace. Here the instructor explains that he wants the ride to keep one horse's length between horses for the sake of good order, and to prove to him that each rider is in control of his horse, and these facts must be explained to the class.

Once the class is walking on at the correct distances it must be taught how to ride through the corners of the school, going as far as possible into the corner without going so deep that it upsets the horse's balance or spoils the pace. Frequent changes of rein must be made; the simplest way to introduce the class to changing the rein is by inclining across the diagonal from quarter marker to quarter marker (Fig. 3).

This initial period in walk serves to warm up both horses and riders. The instructor must pay strict attention to warming up, particularly with unfit riders or when the weather is cold. He should also use this period for the correction of individual riders' positions and the application of the aids. He should never address his remarks privately, to one person; he can refer to any individual, but he should speak so that the whole class can hear. Very often he will find that one member of his class requires much more attention than the others, and great care must be taken here to ensure that this extra attention is not given at the expense of the other pupils.

When he is about to work the class in trot, the instructor must prepare them correctly. He must remind the class that the horses should be walking actively and that the reins must be shortened a little so that they are the correct length when the horse is in trot. A suitable word of command here would be 'Prepare to trot rising — is your walk sufficiently active? — will your reins be the right length when you are trotting? — ride *ter-rot.*' The lengthening of the word trot will be understood by the school horses and will help the riders with the transitions.

At a later stage this command can be reduced to 'Prepare to trot rising — ride trot.' If the school horses are very responsive to the instructor's words of command in transitions both up and down, he must do something to disguise his words of command lest the horses respond more quickly than the rider applies the aids. This is often the case, and of course does not improve the rider's aids. To overcome this problem the instructor may choose to say 'Prepare to trot rising — trot *now.*' This may disguise his intention from the horse and put the onus entirely on the rider to make the transition by the correct application of the aids. Once the class is trotting the instructor can work on improving each rider's position in rising trot.

Improving the rising trot is difficult for some riders. It must be explained to them that the shape of the body and the position of the legs and hands is exactly the same as in walk or sitting trot. The only difference is that the top part of the body is inclined slightly forward from the hips, and not from the waist, as this rounds the back. The shoulders lead the movement and rise slightly over the hands. It is not a question of standing up and sitting down, but of lifting the seat out of the saddle and lowering it down again under control. It should be made clear to the rider that if he sits in the correct position and is supple, the movement of the horse will throw him up sufficiently and that no real physical effort is required on his part. In fact too much physical effort on the part of the rider will spoil the rising trot. All that the rider is required to do is to remain supple in the elbows and the shoulders so that his body can go up and down without moving his hands. He should lift his seat out of the saddle with his hips and shoulders parallel to the horse's shoulders and lower the seat down onto the saddle again with equal weight on each seat bone. This explanation is not intended to be a lesson in how the rising trot should be made but rather to suggest to the instructor some ways in which he can put this subject over to his pupils.

There are many school exercises that can be made in both walk and trot. These exercises are designed to enable the instructor to involve the whole class in maximum activity whilst keeping good control and making individual corrections to the riders. These exercises should be carefully explained to the class and practised first in walk and then in trot.

Changing the rein across the diagonal (Fig. 3)
The command, given as the leading file passes the 'F' marker on the right rein, is 'In single file at "K" right incline and change the rein, through "M".'

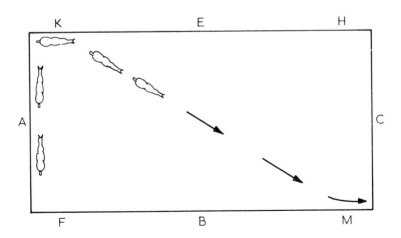

Fig 3 In single file at K right incline and change the rein through M

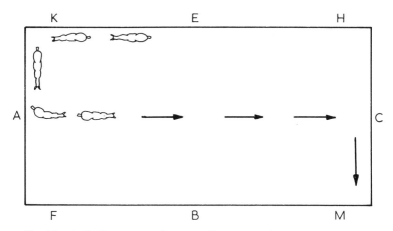

Fig 4 In single file turn up the centre line at A and change the rein at C

Changing the rein up the centre line (Fig. 4)
The command is given as the leading file passes the 'E' marker
on the left rein, 'In single file turn up the centre line at "A"
and at "C" change the rein.'

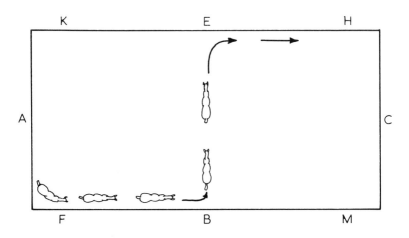

Fig 5 In single file at B turn left and change the rein at E

Changing the rein by turning across the school (Fig. 5)
The command is given to the class as the leading file passes 'A'
on the left rein, 'In single file at "B" left turn and change the
rein at "E".'

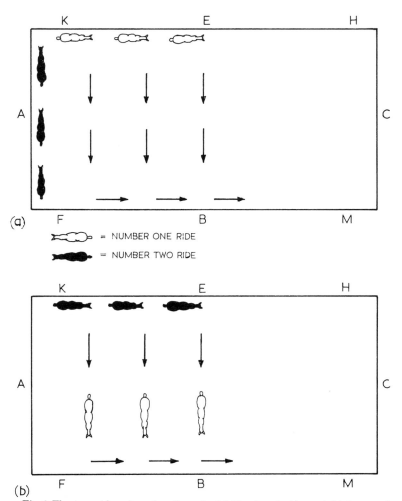

Fig 6 The two rides changing the rein: (a) Number 1 ride — right turn and change the rein; (b) Number 2 ride — right turn and change the rein

Changing the rein by rides (Figs. 6a, b)

The command is given as the leading file passes 'B' on the right rein, 'Numbers 1 to 4 are number one ride and the remainder are number two ride.' Then as the leading file approaches 'E', 'Number one ride right turn and change the rein' and as the leading file of number two ride approaches 'E', 'Number two ride right turn and change the rein.'

This exercise will encourage precise, accurate riding as one ride. The riders must turn together and must ride across the school at right angles maintaining their spacing and dressing. The leading file of number two ride must not drift inwards to follow number one ride, but must continue straight down the long side of the school until he receives the command to turn.

Circle right or circle left (Figs. 7a, b, c, d)
The command is given as the leading file approaches the 'K' marker on the left rein, 'Number one ride circle left', whereupon each rider in number one ride makes a half circle on to the centre line so that number one ride forms a single file down the centre line towards 'C' with number 4 as leading file. As the first rider in number two ride approaches the 'K' marker the command is given, 'Number two ride circle left.' Number two ride performs the same exercise so that the whole ride is moving down the centre line in single file towards 'C'. As the leading rider in number one ride approaches 'G' the command is given, 'Number one ride away', each member of number one ride makes a half circle to the right back on to the track, so that they arrive back on the track in their original order. As the first rider in number two ride approaches 'G' the command is given, 'Number two ride away', number two ride make individual half circles to the right so that they arrive back on the track in their original order and the whole ride is back on the track on the right rein in its correct order.

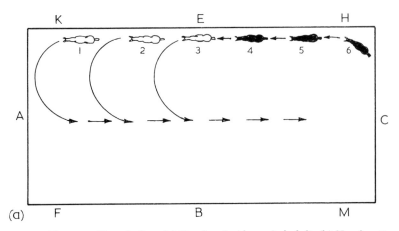

(a)

Fig 7 The two rides circling: (a) Number 1 ride — circle left; (b) Number 2 ride — circle left; (c) Number 1 ride — ride away; (d) Number 2 ride — ride away

(b)

(c)

(d)

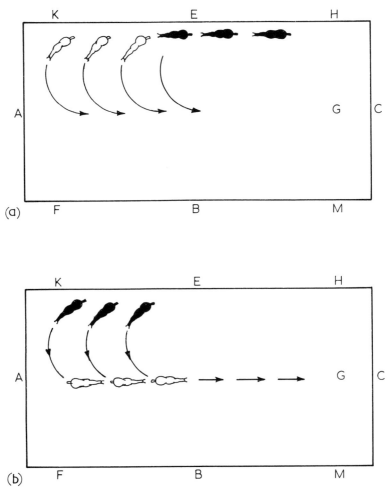

(a)

(b)

Fig 8 The two rides performing the half figure of eight: (a) Number 1 ride — half figure of eight; (b) Number 2 ride — half figure of eight

The half figure of eight (Figs. 8a, b, c, d)
The command is given as the leading file reaches the 'K' marker on the left rein, 'Number one ride half figure of eight.' Number one ride performs exactly the same exercise as in circling to the right, and continues in single file down the centre line towards 'C' with rider number 4 leading. As the leading file of number two ride approaches the 'K' marker the command is given 'Number two ride half figure of eight' and number two ride makes the same exercise circling right and

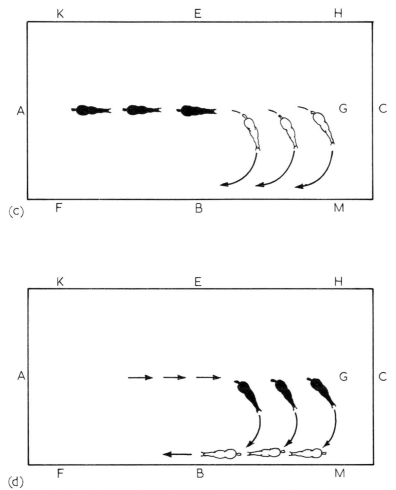

Fig 8 (c) Number 1 ride — ride away; (d) Number 2 ride — ride away

continuing down the centre line, in single file towards 'C', in line with number one ride. As the leading rider (number 4) approaches 'G' the command is given, 'Number one ride away.' Here number one ride make individual half circles to the right back on to the track with rider number 1 in leading file so changing the rein. As the leading rider in number two ride approaches 'G' the command is given, 'Number two ride away' and number two ride make individual half circles back on to the track to the right so forming single file on the track with rider number 5 leading behind number one ride.

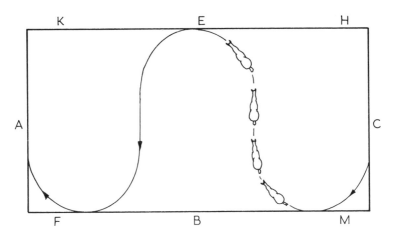

Fig 9 In single file from C make three serpentine loops the full width of the school, finishing at A

The three loop serpentine (Fig. 9)
The command for this exercise is given as the leading file passes 'B' on the right rein. 'In single file from "C" make three serpentine loops, the full width of the school, finishing at "A".'

Forming a double ride (Figs. 10, 11, 12)
The command is given on either rein as the leading file passes the 'E' or 'B' marker. 'The leading file turn down the centre at "A" (or "C") and at "C" (or "A") odd numbers to the right even numbers to the left form a double ride.'

Most of the exercises that are made as a single ride can be made as a double ride. This work is useful as it encourages the riders to ride with more precision and increases their awareness of other riders. It also adds variation to the school work and is usually enjoyed by the class.

The ride on the right rein is responsible for the pace and the ride on the left rein is responsible for the dressing.

When the two rides meet on the track they pass left hand to left hand.

(*opposite top*) Fig 10 Forming a double ride — at A the odd numbers turn right and the even numbers turn left

(*opposite centre*) Fig 11 The ride on the right rein is responsible for the pace and the ride on the left rein is responsible for the dressing

(*opposite below*) Fig 12 The two rides pass left hand to left hand at C

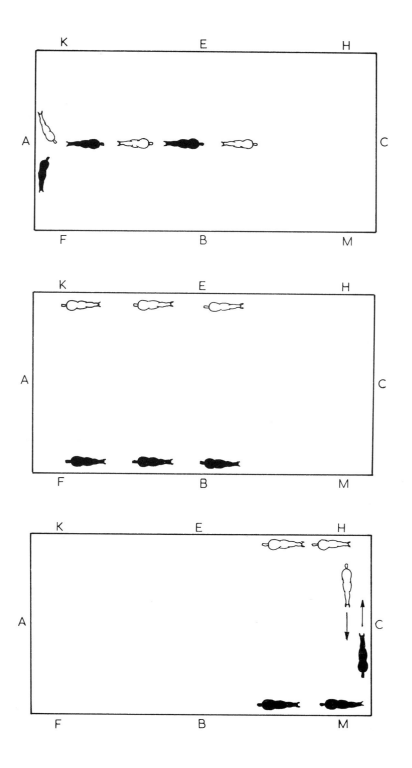

Figures 13–16 show a selection of useful exercises for a double ride.

These exercises can be made on the left or the right rein but sufficient warning should be given by a cautionary word of command to allow the riders to prepare themselves before the executive word of command is given.

This type of class activity can easily be made into a show or demonstration. A carefully planned programme, ridden to music, can be enjoyed by both participants and spectators alike. As the class improves, work in canter and lateral work can be included.

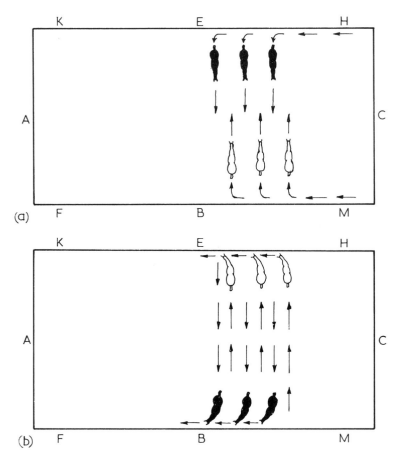

Fig 13 (a) Both rides inwards turn; (b) ...and change the rein

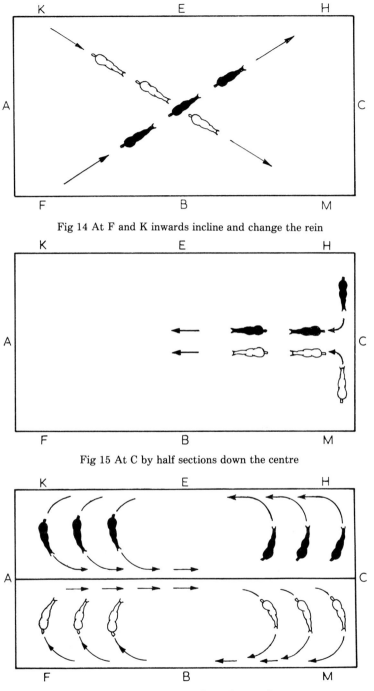

Fig 14 At F and K inwards incline and change the rein

Fig 15 At C by half sections down the centre

Fig 16 Both rides inwards circle — and away

Riding on the correct diagonal in trot

As the student's understanding of riding improves he must be taught to ride on a given diagonal in rising trot.

Firstly, the rhythm of trot and the sequence in which the horse's hooves come to the ground must be explained. This can be done convincingly by demonstrating with a horse that has diagonally opposite white legs, the other pair being coloured or, failing this, by fitting red bandages to the near fore and off hind and white bandages to the off fore and near hind. This will make the sequence in which the hooves strike the ground in trot obvious to the class.

Once the instructor has explained that the horse's feet come to the ground in diagonally opposite pairs in two time it will be easy for the rider to understand that in rising trot he lifts his seat out of the saddle as one diagonal pair come to the ground and lowers it onto the saddle as the other diagonal pair come to the ground, thereby producing the 'one-two' rhythm of rising trot.

To enable the rider to identify the diagonal on which he is riding, he should be made to count out loud the rhythm of trot as he rides along in rising trot. He should then change from counting 'one-two', to 'up-down'. He should then be told to look down at the horse's outside shoulder, and as the shoulder comes back he should lower his seat to the saddle. In this way he will lower his seat to the saddle as the outside foreleg and inside hindleg come to the ground together, and lift his seat out of the saddle as the inside foreleg and outside hindleg come to the ground. He can be taught to identify the diagonal on which he is riding by looking down at the inside shoulder and lifting his seat out of the saddle as the inside shoulder comes back. This will achieve the same result, but is usually found to be less easy to pick up than lowering the seat to the saddle on the outside diagonal.

Once the student can successfully identify the diagonal on which he is riding it is only a short step to being able to change it when necessary. This is best achieved by getting him to say 'up-down-up-down' in rhythm with the stride and to sit for two beats saying 'down-down' as he. does so. When this is thoroughly mastered, the rider has made real progress along the road to understanding what is happening underneath him when he rides.

Riding without stirrups

Riding without stirrups is one of the most important aspects of all the rider's training. It develops confidence and plays a major part in establishing a deep supple seat. This work is best carried out in a dressage saddle to enable the rider to sit deep and to allow the leg to be long. The jumping or general purpose saddle is not entirely suitable for this training as the seat of the saddle tends to be longer and shallower and the rider's leg, if allowed to be long, tends to come off the back of the saddle flap with the bottom of the flap catching on the top of the rider's boot. This work is best done by removing the stirrups and leathers from the saddle altogether, but this is time consuming and inconvenient. If the stirrup leathers are crossed over the saddle carelessly causing a lump of twisted leather under the rider's thigh he will be uncomfortable and may sit on the back of the saddle to avoid the discomfort. This defeats the object of riding without stirrups. The stirrup leather buckles should therefore be pulled down so that the leathers can be folded flat across the saddle, avoiding any uncomfortable bump under the rider's leg.

All the work normally done with stirrups can eventually be done without, but the instructor should remember the effect that too much sitting trot of a poor quality may have on his horses. The horses used for class instruction at this level will probably be hollow and unlikely to accept the rider's hand, and too much novice sitting trot may tend to make them even more hollow.

Initially this work will be tiring for the rider as he will probably tend to grip up and tense the muscles of the leg and upper body. He must be encouraged to relax and be at rest in the bottom of the saddle. Whilst as much of the inside of the rider's leg as possible must stay in contact with the saddle and the horse's side, he must not be allowed to grip as this will tend to squeeze him up and out of the saddle.

To help the riders to sit deep in sitting trot they should be told to take both reins and the whip in the outside hand, and to loop one finger of the inside hand under the pommel of the saddle. In this way they can give themselves a pull down into the saddle and they are usually surprised at how much closer they can sit when doing this.

Rising trot without stirrups should not be taught to the

novice rider as it tends to make him grip up and shorten his legs. It is, however, an excellent strengthening exercise for the competitive cross-country rider, point-to-pointer and polo player, and will be covered later in this book.

Teaching the aids
Teaching the correct way to apply the aids is perhaps the most difficult problem confronting the riding instructor. Most beginners start riding thinking that to make a horse go you kick him, to make him stop you pull on both reins, to turn right you pull the right rein and to turn left you pull the left rein. Unfortunately, where the beginner has had some experience on an untrained horse and perhaps under the guidance of an unskilled adviser, this is often the case.

However, the basic principles of the application of the aids must be clearly instilled in the student from the start. He must be taught to ride with a sure rein contact. It is desirable that one should ride with a light rein, but it is much more desirable that one should ride with a sure, steady, even but 'allowing' contact through the rein to the horse's mouth.

The rider should somehow be made to understand that the aids with legs, seat and hands are private and confidential signals sent by the rider to the horse, and that they should hardly be visible to the spectator. When applying any aids the rider should have two fundamental requirements in mind: firstly, that he wants maximum response from the horse with minimum effort on the part of the rider, and secondly, that he should aim at one aid achieving one response.

It is very easy to teach the rider the effect of using the left rein or the right rein, or the left leg or the right leg; what is difficult is to teach him how much to use of each and in what blend or combination. This is a question of feel, and is dependent upon the pupil's imagination and genius as a rider being carefully developed and guided by an expert instructor. Many pianists learn to read music and to strike the correct notes on the piano. Few arrive on the concert platform because the majority have insufficient 'feel' to produce from the piano the full potential of the music. This theory very much applies to the riding of horses.

The basic theory of the classical application of the aids *must* be understood by the student, and is as follows:

The inside leg creates impulsion.
The outside leg controls the quarters and asks for canter.
The inside hand asks for the bend.
The outside hand controls the speed, the impulsion and the bend in the neck.

The hand aids are made by a 'take and give' feeling with the fingers, as though the rider were holding a rubber squash ball in his hand and squeezing it. This aid will only have an effect if the rein contact is correct.

The leg aids to ask the horse to go forward are applied by closing the leg directly inwards, not by swinging the leg backwards and upwards as is so often seen. If the correct leg aid does not achieve the required response then it should not be increased but must be repeated correctly and reinforced with the whip.

This is not intended to be a chapter on the correct application of the aids, but is meant to explain to the instructor that he will have to be versatile in his teaching of the aids and make adaptations to suit the situation. For instance, where one is confronted with a class of novice children on equally novice ponies and instruction is to take place on a wild hillside in March, little progress will be made if the class is asked to move off into walk by closing the inside leg lightly against the pony's side, whilst keeping a sure, steady, even rein contact. It will probably be necessary to say, 'close both legs strongly against the pony's sides two or three times and lighten the rein a little.' This is clearly not correct riding, but to be a competent instructor one has to be versatile and adapt one's principles to obtain a result.

When teaching the thoughtful pupil the correct application of the aids, the question of 'the five basic rein effects' is bound to be raised at some stage. This theory is taught in some very successful schools and is supported by many serious teachers of riding. The instructor should have a thorough understanding of this principle in order to be able to teach it or refute it, depending on his own convictions. Figure 17 shows how two leading authorities illustrate this principle. There is, however, a strong school of thought that the aids made with the reins are less complicated than this.

The complete rider will be able to apply the aids classically and correctly, and will be able to use legs, back, seat and hands

REIN OF INDIRECT OPPOSITION IN FRONT OF WITHERS
For sharp turn, while moving or for turn on centre in place

Direction

Left hand moves to right rear across the neck

Right hand is passive, or may act to hurry turn

Legs act to control turn either on centre or on haunches

REIN OF DIRECT OPPOSITION
For sharp turn, while moving or turn on centre in place

Direction

Left hand exerts slight tension to rear

3

Right hand yields or is passive

Left leg maintains pace

Right leg is passive at girth or moves back slightly to resist croup swinging out

NECK REIN
For change of direction without change of pace

Direction

4

Left hand raised and with no tension to rear, presses rein against neck

Right hand is passive or may apply leading rein

Legs maintain pace

REIN OF INDIRECT OPPOSITION IN REAR OF WITHERS
For right turn, while moving

2

Left hand moves to right rear but not across neck

Direction

Right hand is passive

Left leg pushes croup to right

Right leg is passive

LEADING REIN
For turn on large curve

Direction

Left hand moves out to side with no rearward tension on rein

5

Right hand, held low, is passively yielding, as horse turns head or resists overbending

Left leg maintains pace

Right leg passive, or may act behind girth to sharpen turn

(*above and opposite*) Fig 17 Two different schools of thought showing the five basic rein effects

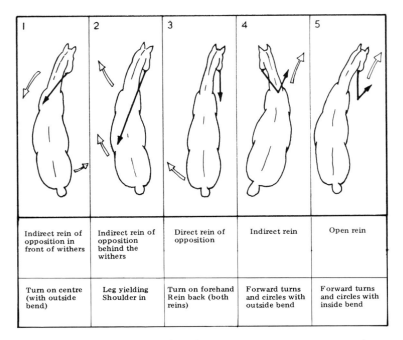

1	2	3	4	5
Indirect rein of opposition in front of withers	Indirect rein of opposition behind the withers	Direct rein of opposition	Indirect rein	Open rein
Turn on centre (with outside bend)	Leg yielding Shoulder in	Turn on forehand Rein back (both reins)	Forward turns and circles with outside bend	Forward turns and circles with inside bend

strongly and effectively in an emergency or where circumstances require it. The riding instructor must understand this and should educate his students along these lines, being careful to note when they reach a stage of riding and horse understanding at which they can absorb and appreciate this more sophisticated attitude towards the aids.

Mounted exercises to improve the rider's confidence, suppleness, balance and co-ordination

These exercises can be done at halt, walk, trot or canter both in a ride or on the lunge, and should be introduced to the student progressively through the paces.

When the exercises are carried out in a class lesson, and on the move, a reliable leading file is required who will not perform the exercises but will set a steady pace for the ride to follow.

Each rider should tie a knot in the reins so that they can be dropped on the horse's neck, and the whips should either be taken from the class by the instructor or be held by the rider between the thigh and the saddle. These exercises can be made with or without stirrups, and when made at trot are best made in sitting trot.

Fig 18 Mounted exercises to improve the rider's balance and agility:
(a) Swinging both arms together in a half circle; (b) A trunk twisting exercise,
first to the left and then to the right; (c) Alternate arm swinging; (d)
Stretching the right hand down towards the right toe; (e) Stretching the right
hand down towards the left toe; (f) Swinging the body both backwards and
forwards

A selection of mounted exercises are shown in Figure 18.

a) Swinging the arms together in a half circle. Here the rider
raises both arms up above his head and swings them down and
up together, in a rhythmical and relaxed manner.

b) Trunk twisting to the left and to the right. The arms are held
out level with the shoulders and the top part of the body is
swung rhythmically from left to right and right to left,
twisting at the waist.

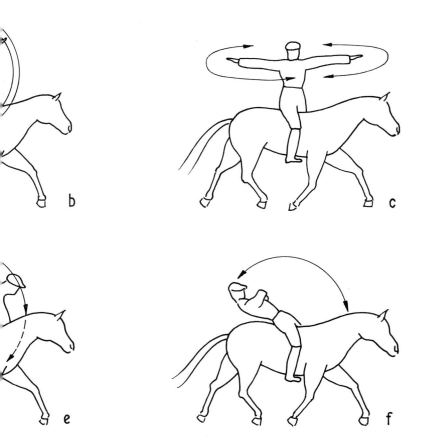

c) Alternate arm swinging. Here the arms are swung from front to rear alternately.

d) Right hand down towards right toe, or left hand down towards left toe. The arms are held out level with the shoulders and the rider leans forward to touch the right toe with the right hand, or the left toe with the left hand.

e) Right hand down towards left toe or left hand down towards right toe. Instructions are the same as for the previous exercise, but the rider reaches across his horse's neck to touch the opposite toe.

f) Body swinging backwards and forwards. With the arms lightly folded the rider swings the upper body forwards and backwards continuing to look ahead.

Above all suppleness and rhythm must be maintained and the seat and legs kept in the correct position.

The class lesson for the more advanced riders

When taking a class of novice riders, the instructor uses the class to obtain good control and maximum activity from each rider. As students progress the practice of riding one behind the other in a ride at one horse's distance becomes less suitable. Both horses and riders will progress at different rates, so it will be necessary for the instructor to vary the training programme and the exercises for each rider.

It is possible for up to eight experienced riders to work individually in a riding school carrying out their own programme of work, provided that a few basic rules are observed.

a) Normal gentlemanly conduct and good manners are the first priority.

b) When riders meet head on they pass left hand to left hand.

c) The rider making the more advanced exercise has priority.

d) When in walk one works on the inside track (about 1.5m in from the wall).

e) Transitions down, whenever possible, are made across the A-C line.

f) Conversations — other than those directly connected with the work in hand — are not permitted.

g) Riders who wish to halt to rest do so across the A-C line.

h) No rider dismounts or leaves the school without the permission of the instructor.

i) Great care is taken in the use of the whip as a punishment, in case other horses or riders are startled by such action.

In this way the instructor can set the programme of work for each pupil or group of pupils and can give individual instructions as required.

In order to create greater control and to give some variety to this work it is sometimes helpful to divide the class into two halves and work each half on a large circle, one half at 'A' and the other half at 'C'. The four riders in each ride space themselves out so that there is an equal distance between them (Fig. 19). An important part of this exercise is that the riders should keep the correct distance between each other, not by making the circle smaller or by spoiling its shape by going further into the corner, but by maintaining the correct circle and lengthening or shortening the steps as necessary.

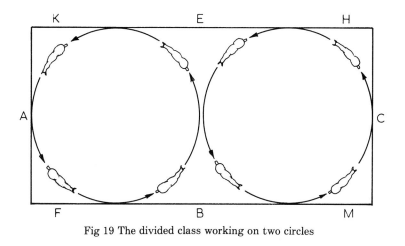

Fig 19 The divided class working on two circles

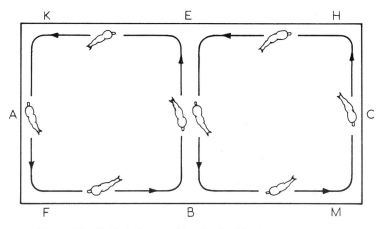

Fig 20 The divided class working in shoulder-in on two squares

To help the riders to do this, 'circle points' should be marked on the wall to show each rider where he should 'brush' the track when making a true circle. This 'circle point' is midway between 'B' or 'E' and the corner of the school (Fig. 2). The circle can be changed to a square (Fig. 20), and to a diamond shape (Fig. 21) to enable work on precision riding and suppling exercises for the horse.

Transitions can be made up and down through halt, walk, trot, canter and rein back as a class on the instructor's word of command. Work can include collected, working and medium

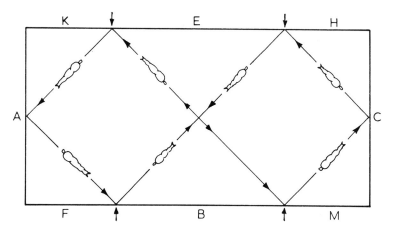

Fig 21 The divided class working on two diamonds

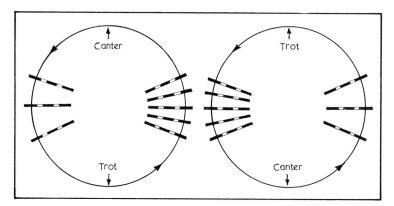

Fig 22 Trotting and cantering poles positioned on the circle

paces with the exception of medium canter. Shoulder-in, travers, renvers, half-pirouettes and turns on the forehand can all be worked on under these circumstances.

Trotting poles can be introduced into each circle, as can cantering poles. Both trotting poles and cantering poles can be positioned at opposite sides of the circle so that the riders trot one half of the circle and canter the other half, making correct transitions on the circle (Fig 22).

It is not necessary to have both rides working on the same rein; the ride at the 'A' end of the school may be on the right rein and the ride at the 'C' end of the school on the left rein. Changing the rein may be carried out in a variety of ways.

a) By turning down the centre line 'A' to 'C' or 'C' to 'A' and re-establishing the circle on the new rein at the opposite end of the school.

b) By inclining across the diagonal, passing left hand to left hand at 'X' and re-establishing the circle on the new rein at the opposite end of the school.

c) By a half-pirouette in walk.

d) By a turn on the forehand.

4
Teaching Riding on the Lunge

Training on the lunge is of immense value to all riders, from beginners to Grand Prix competitors. For the beginner it is a good introduction to the horse, giving him confidence and helping him to develop his seat, and this was discussed in some detail in Chapter 2. For the improving rider it deepens his seat and hence improves his feel of correct paces, and most important of all through the transitions. For the advanced rider it is a useful exercise for revision and correction. Even the most talented and successful riders slip into bad habits, and need to return to school from time to time.

The basic principles of lungeing the horse for training the rider are the same at all levels. The horse must be correctly dressed and must be of suitable temperament for the task. For the beginner rider it is sufficient that the horse should be safe, obedient and comfortable. Safety is a fundamental factor; the horse must not shy or take fright under any circumstances but always remain placid and calm. A lunge horse that gives the beginner rider a fright by shying or running off will do very much more harm than good. It is not therefore necessary that this horse is an extravagant mover. It is better that he should walk and trot at a calm steady pace, obedient to the instructor's command. It is unlikely, although not impossible, that this horse will be able to work on the lunge at canter sufficiently slowly to be of value to the beginner.

The horse that is used for the improving or the advanced rider is a quite different animal. He must be capable of going correctly in walk, trot and canter, on the bit and in the correct outline. He must be capable of making good transitions both between and within the paces, and he must have good balance and impulsion.

The horse and rider properly equipped for lungeing (*Author*)

Warming up on the lunge before the side reins are fitted (*Author*)

When lungeing the more advanced rider on this horse the side reins are made a little shorter, as the horse will be working in a more rounded outline, and the stirrups and leathers should be removed from the saddle altogether. If the rider can ride long enough without stirrups however, but finds difficulty riding long enough with them, they should be retained.

Although the beginner was introduced to rising trot on the lunge this was for practical convenience only, and there is no place for this exercise for the competent rider. The main value of training on the lunge for the advanced rider is to correct and improve the seat and to blend the movement of the rider's body into the movement of the horse through transitions and variations of pace.

The truly expert instructor will place great value on a good lunge horse. He should not be confined to a life of 15m circles on side reins. He is often a senior member of the stable who has proved himself capable of playing this very important role. A hack in the country or an hour or two each day in the field will be sufficient to keep him fresh and rewarded.

To lunge any rider successfully the instructor must be able to lunge his horse correctly, maintaining correct speed, rhythm and impulsion in each pace. At the same time he must devote

Lungeing the horse and rider at walk (*By courtesy of the British Horse Society*)

The dangers of poor lungeing. The slack lunge rein is caught up in the hind leg (*Findlay Davidson*)

most of his attention to the rider, quickly identifying faults and problems and suggesting remedial exercises.

The standard of lungeing must be exemplary. The instructor must stand still in the centre of the circle to ensure that the circle is round, and must keep a sure contact through an untwisted rein with the spare end looped tidily in his hand. The whip must be used carefully and correctly, towards the horse's hindquarters to increase the speed or impulsion and to send him forward, or towards the shoulder to keep him out on the circle. The whip under these circumstances must never startle the horse or make him jump. Frequent changes of rein must be made to ensure equal development of both horse and rider.

Thirty to forty minutes on the lunge is sufficient time for any rider to achieve maximum benefit from this exercise. The observant instructor will identify the moment when the pupil is at his best, and this is the time to stop as deterioration may follow. Whenever possible, all training should end on a good note.

5
Teaching
the Dressage Rider

The complete riding instructor will understand that riders fall into two broad classes: those who wish to use the horse as a means of transport, and those who wish to train their horses for any branch of equitation, along classical lines and to the limits of the horse's physical and mental capabilities. Neither of these groups should be ignored or decried by the professional instructor.

The first group will want their horses to be willing and obedient, to start and stop when required, to turn left and right and to jump. They may not be particular as to exactly how these ends are achieved, and will probably not be sufficiently skilled riders to obtain results without the use of various bits, martingales and other artificial aids. It is essential that the riding instructor understands the requirements of this branch of the riding fraternity and that he is an expert in the use of martingales, schooling martingales, draw and running reins and various types of popular bits.

Many of these riders are excellent horsemasters and stable managers who derive a great deal of enjoyment from their horses. They will often come to a riding instructor for help, and he must understand their attitude to riding and be able to assist them. On the other hand, there are those riders who wish to train their horses along classical lines without force or compulsion, but by the gradual and progressive development of the horse's physical and mental qualities. It is these riders and their horses that will be considered in this chapter.

Any horse can be trained as a dressage horse, but some are very much more rewarding than others because they have natural elegance, balance and quality of paces. Exactly the same applies to riders; they can all be trained as dressage riders but some are so much better suited than others because of their shape, elegance and temperament.

Probably the greatest problem that the instructor will face is training the novice rider who comes to him on an untrained horse. Provided that the horse has not been spoiled previously this combination can be a most rewarding challenge. Under these circumstances three major courses of action must be followed:

a) The pupil must work on his own horse under instruction.
b) He must be trained on a well schooled horse from time to time so that he knows what he is aiming for.
c) The instructor must ride the pupil's horse to help put him on the right lines and to assess any difficulties that the horse may have and with which his pupil will have to cope.

The pupil must understand his ultimate aim clearly, and it should be reduced to as few words as possible. Once he realises

The collected walk. Harry Boldt of West Germany on Woyceck (*Findlay Davidson*)

that he is trying to put the horse in a position where he, the horse, can improve his own natural paces and outline, the pupil will be well on the way to understanding the true aim of dressage training. The Rules of the International Equestrian Federation state the following:

'The object of Dressage is the harmonious development of the physique and ability of the horse. As a result it makes the horse calm, supple, loose and flexible, but also confident, attentive and keen, thus achieving perfect understanding with his rider.

These qualities are revealed by:

the freedom and regularity of the paces;
the harmony, lightness and ease of the movements;
the lightness of the forehand and the engagement of the hindquarters, originating in a lively impulsion;
the acceptance of the bridle, with submissiveness throughout and without any tenseness or resistance.

The horse thus gives the impression of doing of his own accord what is required of him. Confident and attentive he submits generously to the control of his rider, remaining absolutely straight in any movement on a straight line and bending accordingly when moving on curved lines.

His walk is regular, free and unconstrained. His trot is free, supple, regular, sustained and active. His canter is united, light and cadenced. His quarters are never inactive or sluggish. They respond to the slightest indication of the rider and thereby give life and spirit to all the rest of his body.

By virtue of a lively impulsion and the suppleness of his joints, free from the paralysing effects of resistance, the horse obeys willingly and without hesitation and responds to the various aids calmly and with precision, displaying a natural and harmonious balance both physically and mentally.

In all his work, even at the halt, the horse must be 'on the bit'. A horse is said to be 'on the bit' when the hocks are correctly placed, the neck is more or less raised and arched according to the stage of training and the extension or collection of the pace, and he accepts the bridle with a light and soft contact and submissiveness throughout. The head should remain in a steady position, as a rule slightly in front of the vertical, with a supple poll as the highest point of the neck, and no resistance should be offered to the rider.'

Teaching the paces

Before the student of dressage attempts to have any effect on his horse he must understand the basic requirements of each of the horse's paces.

When teaching the timing and sequence of the paces, it is clearer if one refers to inside legs and outside legs rather than to left and right or to near and off. The inside legs are those on the concave side of the horse and the outside legs are those on the convex side. Consequently the inside legs are not necessarily those on the inside of the arena; for instance, a horse in counter canter will be bent away from the centre of the arena, and therefore if his inside legs are on his concave side they are on the outside of the arena.

There are four recognised types of walk: collected walk, medium walk, extended walk and free walk. The walk is a marching pace in which the footfalls of the horse's feet follow one another in 'four time', well marked and maintained in all

The collected walk. Dr Reiner Klimke of West Germany on Anlerich (*Findlay Davidson*)

work at the walk. The sequence of footfalls is firstly outside
hind, then outside fore, inside hind and finally inside fore.
When the four beats cease to be distinctly marked, even and
regular, the walk is disunited or broken.

It is at the pace of walk that the imperfections of dressage
are most evident, and this is also the reason why a horse
should not be asked to walk 'on the bit' at the early stages of
his training. Any attempt to quicken collection before the
horse is ready will spoil not only the collected walk, but the
medium and the extended walk as well.

The trot, always with free, active and regular steps, should
be moved into without hesitation. It is a pace in two time when
the feet come to the ground in diagonally opposite pairs,
outside hind and inside fore together, followed by the inside
hind and outside fore together. There is a period of suspension
between each pair coming to the ground when in fact no feet
are on the ground.

Free walk on a long rein. Dr Reiner Klimke of West Germany on Mehmed
(*Findlay Davidson*)

The quality of the trot is judged by the general impression given, the regularity and elasticity of the steps — originating from a supple back and well engaged hindquarters — and by the ability of maintaining the same rhythm and natural balance.

The following trots are recognised: collected trot, working trot, medium trot and extended trot.

During collected trot, the horse, remaining 'on the bit', moves forward with his neck raised and arched. The hocks, being well engaged, maintain an energetic impulsion, thus enabling the shoulders to move with greater ease in any direction. The horse's steps are shorter than in the other trots, but he is lighter and more mobile.

Working trot is a pace between the collected and the medium trot, in which a horse, not yet trained and ready for collected movements, shows himself properly balanced and, remaining 'on the bit', goes forward with even elastic steps and good hock

The collected trot. Christine Stuckelberger of Switzerland on Granat (*Findlay Davidson*)

The extended trot. Christine Stuckelberger of Switzerland on Granat (*Findlay Davidson*)

(*opposite above*) The extended trot. Dr Uwe Schulten-Baumer of West Germany on Madras (*Findlay Davidson*)

(*opposite below*) The extended trot. Dr Reiner Klimke of West Germany on Mehmed (*Findlay Davidson*)

action. The expression 'good hock action' does not mean that collection is a required quality of working trot; it only underlines the importance of an impulsion originated from the activity of the hindquarters.

Medium trot is a pace between the working and the extended trot, but 'rounder' than the latter. The horse goes forward with free and moderately extended steps and an obvious impulsion from the hindquarters. The rider allows the horse, remaining 'on the bit', to carry his head a little more in front of the vertical than at the collected and the working trot, and allows him at the same time to lower his head and neck slightly. The steps should be as even as possible, and the whole movement balanced and unconstrained.

In extended trot, the horse covers as much ground as possible. Maintaining the same rhythm, he lengthens his steps to the utmost which results from great impulsion from the hindquarters. The rider allows the horse, remaining 'on the bit', to lower and extend his neck in order to prevent his action from becoming higher. The fore feet should touch the ground on the spot towards which they are pointing.

Canter is a pace in three time. The outside hindleg starts the pace followed by the inside hind and outside forelegs together, followed by the inside foreleg, which is the leading leg. It should be moved into without hesitation, with light, cadenced and regular strides.

The quality of the canter is judged by the general impression given and the regularity and lightness of the three time pace — originating from the acceptance of the bridle with a supple poll and in the engagement of the hindquarters with an active hock action — and by the ability of maintaining the same rhythm and a natural balance. The horse should remain straight on straight lines.

The following canters are recognised: collected canter, working canter, medium canter and extended canter.

In collected canter, the horse, remaining 'on the bit', moves forward with his neck raised and arched. The collected canter is marked by the lightness of the forehand and the engagement of the hindquarters, i.e. is characterised by supple, free and mobile shoulders and very active quarters. The horse's strides are shorter than at the other canters, but he is lighter and more mobile.

Working canter is a pace between the collected and the medium canter, in which a horse not yet trained and ready for collected movements shows himself properly balanced and, remaining 'on the bit', goes forward with even, light and cadenced strides and good hock action. The expression 'good hock action' does not mean that collection is a required quality of working canter. It only underlines the importance of an impulsion originated from the activity of the hindquarters.

Medium canter is a pace between the working and the extended canter. The horse goes forward with free, balanced and moderately extended strides and an obvious impulsion from the hindquarters. The rider allows the horse, remaining 'on the bit', to carry his head a little more in front of the

The collected canter. Christine Stuckelberger of Switzerland on Granat
(*Findlay Davidson*)

vertical than at the collected and working canter, and allows
him at the same time to lower his head and neck slightly. The
strides should be long and as even as possible, and the whole
movement balanced and unconstrained.

In extended canter the horse covers as much ground as
possible. Maintaining the same rhythm, he lengthens his
stride to the utmost, without losing any of his calmness and
lightness, as a result of great impulsion from the hindquarters.
The rider allows the horse, remaining 'on the bit' to lower and
extend his head and neck with the top of his nose pointing
more or less forward.

(*right*) The elegant French seat. Adjutant Patrick le Rolland of France on Debarras (*Author*); (*below*) The style and grace of the dressage horse and rider. Karin Schulter of West Germany on Mars (*Findlay Davidson*)

The dressage rider must have regular lessons on a horse with good quality paces, so that he can constantly improve his recognition and understanding of correct execution of the different paces. He must vary his work on his horse so that the horse is not always worked in the manege or indoor school. The instructor must ensure that the horse is given a balanced programme of work, both in the riding school and out in the country to refresh the horse and give him some variation.

Once the dressage trainer has established in his pupil an understanding of the qualities that go to produce good walk, trot and canter he must train his pupil to make transitions within the paces. He must make collected, medium and extended walk; collected, working, medium and extended trot and canter, piaffer and passage.

The trainer must explain these differences within each pace to avoid confusion. Whilst the imaginative trainer will find various ways in which to explain ideas and concepts he must, once again, have a clear idea of the International Equestrian Federation's definitions.

The dressage rider's position
The position of the dressage rider is of primary importance for three reasons. First of all to give the horse a balanced load to carry, as a well-balanced load is easier to carry than an unbalanced load; secondly, to enable him to be really effective by the correct application of the aids and thirdly, to enable him to look as elegant as possible.

Ideally, the dressage rider should be slim and have good physical proportions. A long slender leg is an advantage as is a slim body with a naturally elegant carriage. Overweight riders or those with short fat limbs are not well suited to dressage riding.

By studying and analysing the seat and position of the dressage experts, the dressage instructor should develop a clear mental picture of the correct seat of the dressage rider. A clear idea of the correct seat will help him to obtain the best from his pupil, having taken into account any natural limitations brought about by a less than perfect conformation.

To enable the dressage rider to sit in the correct position he must ride in the correct saddle. Money expended on a good dressage saddle which is a perfect fit for both horse and rider is a most rewarding investment (Fig 23). The reins are also an important part of the dressage rider's equipment, and should be narrow, leather reins. Rubber, plaited, nylon or webbing reins are unsuitable for dressage riding, as the feel in the fingers lacks subtlety.

Throughout any movement the dressage rider must give an impression of easy elegance and he must never show any signs of difficulty, frustration or exasperation. The dressage instructor must insist upon this attitude being maintained throughout training.

Fig 23 The different saddles used for jumping and dressage: (a) The jumping saddle; (b) The dressage saddle

Establishing the horse's outline
Before the lesson commences, and whilst the rider is adjusting his tack and mounting, the horse must be made to stand still on the centre line of the school at a correct halt, with all four feet square and with equal weight on each leg.

As in all riding training the lesson must start with a warming up period in which the horse is allowed to walk on a long rein with a low head carriage. He must of course comply with the basic rules in that he must go forward, straight and calm during this warming up period.

After five minutes or so the rider should be told to take up the reins and correct his position. He takes up the rein contact that he intends to keep throughout his ride except during periods of rest. The horse must now work on the bit, and to achieve this the rider must give the horse an acceptable hand; the horse should be allowed to go freely forward and to adjust the height of his head and the length of his neck as he wishes. It must however be made clear to the pupil that the horse's head must not be pulled into position by the use of the hands. The horse must be allowed to adjust the height of his head and the length of his neck whilst given an acceptable hand until the required relaxation is achieved. The horse must not be allowed to bend his neck too much to the left or to the right. The rider should aim at the bend in the neck being the same as the bend in the rest of the body. There should be no bend to the outside and no excessive bend to the inside.

The rider must however keep a sure, steady, even contact as the horse makes these adjustments. The result of this quality of rein contact will be that the horse will be allowed to experiment with the height of his head and length of his neck. Once he discovers that the bit does not cause him any discomfort but stays in a steady contact with the bars of his mouth he will relax the muscles that control the vertebrae of the neck, the axis and atlas joints and his jaw and he will carry his head in a naturally correct position. It is important that the instructor makes this principle clear to his student as, until this situation is achieved, aids with the hands cannot be applied correctly.

Once the rider understands the principle of the rein contact and the horse is accepting his hand he can encourage the horse to increase his impulsion by the use of his leg, reinforced if necessary by the long whip.

In order that the horse increases his impulsion he must bring his hindlegs further under himself. This entails greater flexion of the hip, stifle and hock joints and consequently a lowering of the croup. The lowering of the croup results in a lightening of the forehand and provided that the horse has been able to cope with the increase in impulsion and has remained forward, straight, calm and on the bit, considerable progress has been made towards establishing a correct outline. Where an increase in impulsion results in the horse losing any of the three basic qualities — forward, straight and calm — or causes him to give up his acceptance of the rider's hand, then the increase in impulsion must be given up and the basic requirements re-established.

Teaching feel
It is comparatively easy for the instructor to teach his pupil the principle of applying the aids with the legs, the seat and the hands. The difficulty comes when trying to explain how much of any particular aid should be applied. The rider has very few aids at his disposal with which to ask his horse to perform a wide range of activities, from standing still at halt through walk, trot and canter right up to piaffer and passage. In some cases the aids applied for two very different exercises appear to be identical, for instance, in the aids for canter right and half-pass right. When asking the horse to canter right the rider bends the horse a little to the right, keeps the inside leg at the girth to ask for or to maintain the impulsion, and draws the outside leg back to ask the horse to canter. When asking the horse to half-pass right he bends the horse a little to the right, keeps the inside leg at the girth to ask for or to maintain the impulsion, and draws the outside leg back to ask the horse to move his quarters to the right and so make the half-pass. The aids for these two movements are almost identical, the only difference being the way in which the outside leg is used. In the canter transition it is used as an executive command 'canter now'. In half-pass it is used as a prolonged aid or a series of aids to ask the horse to move his quarters over. The use of these aids and their effectiveness depends on the rider's feel and it is this feel which is difficult to teach.

One of the most useful exercises for improving the rider's 'feel' is to lengthen and shorten the steps. This can be done in walk, trot or canter but is best started in trot where both speed and impulsion are more easy to control. The steps are made shorter by maintaining the impulsion with the leg and decreasing the speed by the use of the outside hand. The correct blend of both leg and hand aids will result in the horse taking shorter steps but maintaining his balance, outline, forward movement and calmness. Too much leg or hand will upset this balance. The ability to achieve this balance of the aids is the rider's 'feel'. To lengthen the steps the rider asks for an increase in impulsion from the leg and allows the horse to take longer steps by lengthening his outline, stretching the head and neck forwards. To achieve long, elegant steps requires considerable 'feel' from the rider in the blend of leg and hand aids increasing the impulsion and controlling the build-up of impulsion with the hand to result in good quality, long steps.

The ability to shorten and lengthen the steps is very much a question of the rider's feel and imagination, and knowledge of the correct aids is a basic requirement; but from there, good quality steps are produced by the rider's 'feel'.

A rider will often find difficulty in maintaining the correct rein contact and whilst it is most desirable that the rein contact should be light, it is much more important that it should be sure, steady and even. It is better that the rider should have a little more weight in his hand and maintain a sure, steady, even contact than that he should have a light rein with a contact that is continually varying.

The reins of the double bridle correctly held (*Author*)

Teaching the rider to use the double-bridle
The dressage rules require that for dressage tests horses should be bitted as follows:

Preliminary and Novice standard: ordinary snaffle.
Elementary standard: ordinary snaffle or simple double-bridle, as specified on the test sheet.
Medium standard: ordinary snaffle or simple double-bridle, as specified on the test sheet.
Advanced standard: simple double-bridle.

So as soon as the rider can ride his horse freely forward in a snaffle with a constant correct outline, and on the bit both when going forward and in lateral movements, he may be introduced to the double-bridle.

At first the rider should be taught the basic way in which to hold four reins, with the bit reins round the third finger of each hand and the bridoon reins round the little finger of each hand. The curb chain should be a link or two longer than normal at first, and whilst the rider is mastering the art of holding four reins there should be little or no contact on the bit rein. As he progresses, the bit rein contact can be taken up and the curb chain correctly adjusted. He must be trained to take up the bit rein and let it out smoothly as required.

'Stiff side' and 'soft side'
It is dangerous for the riding instructor to make generalis-ations but it is fairly safe to say that all horses are more stiff on one rein than the other. Usually a horse is more stiff on the right than on the left, and many reasons have been put forward for this. None of them are convincing, other than that horses are left or right handed, rather like human beings, and few of us are truly ambidextrous. The fact that a horse is more stiff to the right than to the left does not mean that he will find all his work on the right rein more difficult. In fact there are some exercises that he may well find easier to the right than to the left. Shoulder-in is one of these.

From the riding instructor's point of view it is important to identify as soon as possible on which rein the horse is stiff and to know how to plan his work to cope with this difficulty. A horse is usually more stiff in one direction due to physical reasons in that he finds his work in that direction difficult. It is therefore quite wrong to make him work predominantly on his stiff side until he becomes supple. The good trainer will start work in the rein on which the horse finds work easier. As the work improves on that rein he will introduce a little work on the stiff side but before the quality of the work deteriorates or the horse starts to resist he will change back to the easier rein. As he improves on the soft side so he will improve on the stiff side. It is wrong to work him on his stiff side for long periods in the hope that his suppleness will improve.

The Dressage Movements

The riding instructor, having established in his pupil a clear understanding of the requirements of the basic paces, walk, trot and canter, must then introduce him progressively to the dressage movements. This work can conveniently be divided into four aspects:

a) What the movement consists of.
b) How to prepare for it.
c) How to ride it.
d) Common faults encountered in it.

Progressive introduction of the dressage movements may usefully be made as follows:

Halt	Shoulder-in	Half-pass
Transitions	Travers	Flying change
Turns	Renvers	Pirouettes
Circles	Rein back	Piaffer
Serpentines	Simple change	Passage
Leg yielding	Counter canter	

The halt
Whilst the *halt* can hardly be considered as a dressage movement it is a test of the horse's balance and obedience. The rider should be taught the correct aids to ask the horse to come to *halt* and it must be emphasised that a good *halt* will most likely come from a well balanced walk, trot and canter. It is unlikely that the horse will *halt* correctly if the pace from which he is making the *halt* is unbalanced or of poor quality.

The practice of halting incorrectly and then tapping the

horse's legs with the stick to adjust those that are left behind should be discouraged as it is approaching the problem from the wrong end. A good *halt* will only come from a good quality preceding pace and correct application of the aids.

Transitions

The International Equestrian Federation Rules demand that:

> 'The changes of pace and speed should be clearly shown at the prescribed marker; they should be quickly made, yet must be smooth and not abrupt. The rhythm of a pace should be maintained up to the moment when the pace is changed or the horse halts. The horse should remain light in hand, calm and maintain a correct position.
>
> The same applies to *transitions* from one movement to another, for instance, from the passage to the piaffer and vice-versa.'

However, a good *transition* is the joining together of two good quality paces. As both horse and rider improve in the execution of correct basic paces so the *transitions* will improve. In teaching the rider to make *transitions* correctly he must learn that preparation is important and that when making a change of pace the first steps of the new pace can only be as good in quality as the last steps of the old pace. For instance, when making the *transition* from trot to walk the horse should go from a full pace in two-time trot to a full pace in four-time walk; if the quality of the trot is poor, lacking impulsion or unbalanced, then the ensuing walk will be poor.

Downward *transitions* are usually more difficult to make correctly than upward *transitions*. When making downward *transitions* it will often be helpful to make them on a circle or at a corner rather than on the straight.

The aids for each *transition* must be taught and clearly understood by the rider, but having achieved this he must learn that the final result will depend on the way in which he applies those aids on any particular horse. Whilst the aids for any *transition* can be easily understood by most riders, it is the blend of leg, seat and hand aids that achieves a smooth, balanced *transition*. Any aid or combination of aids may be used as and when they are required. However the rider's aim must be to achieve maximum response from the horse from minimum effort on the part of the rider which means that the aids must, eventually, be reduced to the minimum.

Turns

When the horse makes a *turn* the dressage rules demand that:

'He should adjust the bend of his body to the curvature of the line he follows, remaining supple and following the indications of the rider, without any resistance or change of pace, rhythm or speed.

When changing direction at right angles, for instance when riding corners, the horse should describe one quarter of a circle of approximately 6m diameter at collected and working paces, and at medium and extended paces one quarter of a circle of approximately 10m diameter.'

Circles

Making *circles* at walk, trot and canter is a basic requirement of the dressage tests from Preliminary upwards.

The *circle* should have no corners and no flat sides. The horse must be bent throughout his entire length on the circumference of the *circle*. It is clear, therefore, that the novice horse will only be asked to make large *circles* and, as his work progresses and he becomes more advanced, the *circles* that he is asked to make will become smaller. This is because a high degree of suppleness and agility is required to enable a horse to make a circle of 15m or less without losing his outline, tempo, impulsion or the quality of his pace.

Serpentines

Serpentines are demanded in the dressage tests in trot and canter with increasing degrees of difficulty as the tests become more advanced. They are a test of the horse's suppleness and his ability to make flowing, continual changes of direction, changing the bend and at the same time maintaining his balance and correctness of pace.

The work should start in trot and later be made in canter. When making *serpentines* in trot the important point is to change the bend in the horse smoothly to conform with the curve of the *serpentine* track. The rider must apply the aids in good time to avoid upsetting the balance of the horse or interfering with his rhythm and free, forward movement. To discourage the horse from changing direction without changing the bend, the *serpentine* loops should be made somewhat pear shaped to start with, and less pear shaped as the work improves.

Work on *serpentines* should be started by making quite small loops off the track, a little over a metre in length, taking great care to ensure that the bend of the horse stays correct throughout the movement. These loops should be increased until they are made the full 20m width of a dressage arena.

Unless otherwise stated, *serpentines* in canter will include at least one loop in counter-canter, so these cannot be attempted until the canter is short and light enough to make counter-canter correctly and without loss of balance. The same principles apply to making *serpentines* in canter as they do in trot, but the bend in the horse must be maintained towards the leading leg throughout the *serpentine* loops.

When starting the work in canter by making small loops off the long side of the school, the trainer must take care that the hind feet follow in the line of tracks made by the fore feet, and that the horse does not move on two tracks making half-pass off the track and leg yielding back on to the track.

Leg yielding
When this is required as a movement in the dressage test the horse is quite straight, except for a slight bend at the poll, so that the rider is just able to see the supercilliary arch and nostril on the inside. The inside legs pass and cross in front of the outside legs. The horse is looking away from the direction in which he is moving.

Leg yielding on the diagonal The horse is quite straight except for a slight bend at the poll, so that the rider is just able to see the supercilliary arch and nostril of the horse, which looks away from the direction in which he is moving (Fig. 24).

Leg yielding along the wall See the description of leg yielding on the diagonal, and Fig. 25.

This movement is incorporated in the dressage test as a lateral movement which is made at a working pace without any degree of collection.

It is a controversial exercise totally shunned by some trainers but used extensively and with good effect by others.

(opposite) Leg yielding to the left (*By courtesy of the British Horse Society*)

Fig 25 Leg yielding
along the wall

Fig 24 Leg yielding on the diagonal

The advantages and disadvantages of such exercises should be studied by all riding teachers to enable them to form their own principles along firm, well considered lines.

Those who support *leg yielding* do so for the following reasons:

a) As an introductory exercise to sideways and forward movement it is an easy one for the horse to execute.
b) No degree of collection is required, so it can be started earlier than shoulder-in.
c) It has a good suppling effect on the horse.

Those who do not support it are of the opinion that:

a) It is an unattractive exercise, not included in the classical repertoire.
b) The bend in the horse is opposite to the direction in which he is moving.

c) To bend the horse at the poll only may cause him to tilt his head to the left or to the right.

d) It invariably causes problems when the horse is asked to make half-pass as it may encourage the horse to lead with the quarters and have insufficient bend.

When teaching *leg yielding* the instructor must guard against two major faults: firstly he must ensure that the horse is kept quite straight, the only bend being at the poll, and secondly that the rider's leg that is asking the horse to yield is not to be drawn back behind the girth, as this may cause the quarters to lead the movement.

Shoulder-in

The dressage rules describe *shoulder-in* as follows:

> 'The horse is slightly bent round the inside leg of the rider. The horse's inside legs pass and cross in front of the outside legs. The horse is looking away from the direction in which he is moving.

> *Shoulder-in*, if performed in the right way, with the whole horse, from the poll to the tail, slightly bent round the inside leg of the rider, is not only a suppling movement but also a collecting movement, because the horse at every step must move his inside hindleg underneath his body and place it in front of the outside, which he is unable to do without lowering his inside hip.

> *Shoulder-in* is performed 'along the wall' at an angle of about 30° to the direction in which the horse is moving.'

This exercise is one of the riding instructor's closest allies. It has a most profound effect on the horse's suppleness; helps very much in improving collection; is the correct and most effective introduction to lateral work; improves the canter strike-off; helps to straighten the crooked horse and when performed correctly is a graceful and elegant movement to watch. Few movements in equitation can boast such a list of beneficial effects on the horse.

There are however varying views on how this exercise should be performed and once again the riding instructor must have a clear knowledge of each version before he can confidently proceed with teaching *shoulder-in*.

The first school of thought is that the horse should form an angle to the track of about 30° with his hips at an angle to the wall and both fore and hind inside legs crossing over the

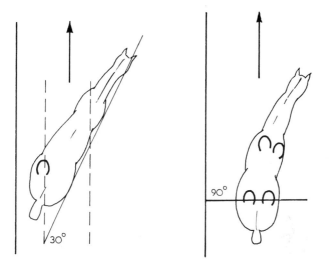

(*left*) Fig 26 The shoulder-in at an angle of 30° with little bend; (*right*) Fig 27 The shoulder-in with the hips positioned at right angles to the track, and bend for a 15 m circle

outside legs. The horse has some consistent bend throughout the length of his body. This is shown quite clearly in the illustration to the dressage rules (Fig. 26). When *shoulder-in* is done in this way there is a tendency for it to be more like leg yielding, particularly if the bend is insufficient or the pace lacks collection.

The alternative view of *shoulder-in* is that the horse's hips should remain at right angles to the wall and that the hind feet should continue straight up the track without crossing or, in fact, making any deviation. The forehand only is taken in and the inside foreleg steps across the outside foreleg. This version requires greater suppleness and bend in the horse and a higher degree of collection, and is shown in Figure 27.

When explaining *shoulder-in* the instructor will have to make clear to his pupil what is meant by one, two, three or four tracks. It is not possible for the rider to see how many tracks he is making as he rides, but he must know the meaning of these expressions so that he can understand the work more clearly and be able to comply with the instructor's wishes.

(*opposite*) The shoulder-in (*By courtesy of the British Horse Society*)

Working on two clear lines of tracks (*By courtesy of the British Horse Society*)

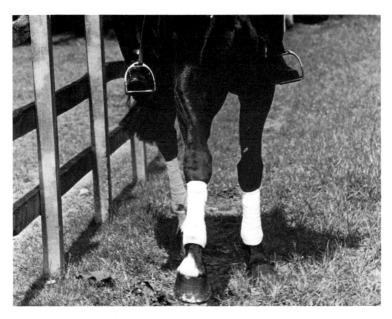

Working on three clear lines of tracks (*By courtesy of the British Horse Society*)

Working on four clear lines of tracks (*By courtesy of the British Horse Society*)

As the horse proceeds along the straight line he makes two lines of foot marks: one track with his outside hind and outside fore, and one track with his inside hind and inside fore. If the forehand is displaced inwards approximately enough to start a 10m circle, a horse will make three tracks: one track with his outside hind foot, a second track with his inside hind foot and outside fore foot and a third track with his inside fore foot.

When the forehand is displaced still further to the inside as if to start a 6m circle the horse will make four lines of tracks: one with his outside hind foot, a second with his inside hind foot, a third with his outside fore foot and a fourth track with his inside fore foot. From this it can be seen that the number of lines of tracks made by the horse's feet depends on the degree of bend in the horse, or the angle of the horse to the wall in the unbent horse (Fig. 28).

When teaching the rider *shoulder-in* it is again a great advantage to give him the opportunity to perform the exercise on a trained horse who will make a correct *shoulder-in* in response to the correct aids. This will give the rider a feel of the blend of the aids required to achieve the exercise. Where this is not possible it is a case of 'the blind leading the blind', but in

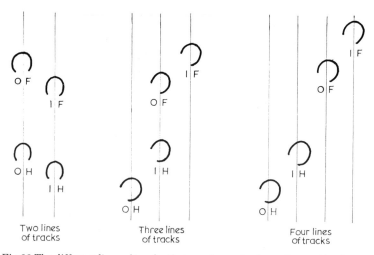

Fig 28 The different lines of tracks that can be made, depending on the degree of bend in the horse

practical, everyday circumstances this is a typical situation with which the riding instructor must learn to cope. Once the pupil fully understands what is required of his horse he must consider carefully the aids that he will use to perform this movement and must go through them in his mind before he attempts to put them into practice on his horse.

A convenient and effective way to introduce this exercise to both horse and rider is to start in walk by making a circle from the half marker on the right rein. Let us say that we plan to make the circle from 'E'. The size of the circle will depend on the degree of training of the horse. It must be as small as he can manage without losing his balance, rhythm, outline, or acceptance of the rider's hand. For the novice horse it may be 15—18m, for the more advanced horse 10—12m and for the advanced horse a volte of 6m.

As the rider completes the circle he continues as though he is going to make a second circle but just as the horse has taken one step off the track with the forehand and the horse's hips have arrived at the 'E' marker, the rider uses the fingers of his outside hand to say 'No — do not go any further forward on the circle', and he may use the outside hand with a slight opening effect to guide the horse along the track. The inside hand maintains the bend to the right, the inside leg is used at the girth to maintain the impulsion, and the outside leg remains in contact ready to prevent the quarters from swinging out. The rider's hips remain parallel to the horse's hips and his shoulders are turned in a little so that they remain parallel to the horse's shoulders. Equal weight is maintained on each seat bone.

If three or four good steps in *shoulder-in* are obtained the horse should be sent energetically forwards, not by taking the forehand back on to the track, but by going forward on the circle made by the bend of the *shoulder-in*. Once satisfactory progress has been made in walk and four or five good quality steps can be made in *shoulder-in* on both reins, then the exercise can be attempted in trot.

Work on this exercise is started in walk as both horse and rider have more time to organise their thoughts and actions. Once they have both begun to understand what is required at walk they should progress to trot, as at trot most horses find the production and maintenance of impulsion easier than at

The Spanish Riding School quadrille performing shoulder-in (*Findlay Davidson*)

The travers (*By courtesy of the British Horse Society*)

walk. *Shoulder-in* must be made with impulsion if it is to play its full part in the further training of horse and rider in which it is so valuable.

Travers

In *travers* the horse is slightly bent round the inside leg of the rider. The horse's outside legs pass and cross in front of the inside legs. The horse is looking in the direction in which he is moving. The exercise is performed 'along the wall' or, preferably, on the centre line, at an angle of about 30° to the direction in which the horse is moving (Fig. 29).

Fig 29 The travers with the shoulders at an angle of 30° to the line of progress

Fig 30 The travers with the shoulders at an angle of 90° to the line of progress and the hind quarters taken in

Travers is an exercise very much akin to shoulder-in. Shoulder-in requires that the forehand is displaced inwards with the front legs crossing over and the quarters remaining square on the track (or nearly so, depending on the horse's development and on the school of thought to which the rider subscribes). *Travers* requires that the hindquarters are displaced inwards and that the forehand stays straight on the track, the hindlegs crossing over and the forelegs continuing to go straight (Fig. 30). The same difference of opinion exists regarding this exercise as in shoulder-in — whether or not the horse should be bent to such a degree that either the hindquarters, in shoulder-in, or the forehand, in *travers*, should be straight on the track with the legs not crossing over, or whether they should be inclined inwards a little, the legs being required to cross over. It will be seen from the definition in the dressage rules that the latter is required in competition. The aids to make *travers*, to comply with either school of thought, are similar and only a question of degree will differentiate between the two.

Travers can be started by asking the pupil to make shoulder-in along the wall, and on arriving at the half marker to circle inwards on a circle commensurate with the bend in his horse. As the horse's shoulders arrive back at the half marker and his head is pointing straight down the track, or nearly so, the rider draws the outside leg back behind the girth to ask the

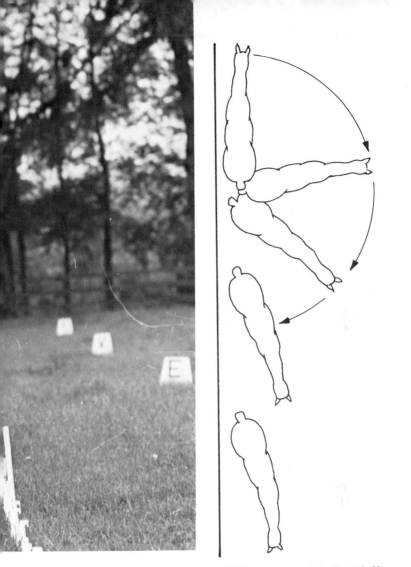

The renvers (explained on the next page) (*By courtesy of the British Horse Society*)

(*right*) Fig 31 The renvers from the half-pirouette in walk

hindquarters to move sideways along the inner track so causing the hindlegs to cross over. The inside leg remains at the girth to maintain the impulsion. The inside hand keeps the bend and asks for the direction whilst the outside hand keeps a contact ready to prevent too great a bend in the neck or an increase in speed. Having completed the required number of steps in *travers* the rider must, with his inside leg, return the horse's hindquarters to the track to let him know that the hindquarters may only be displaced to the left or the right on the clear instruction of the rider.

Renvers
This is exactly the same exercise as travers except that in *renvers* the forehand is brought in from the track, the horse still looking in the direction in which he is moving. Like travers it is a suppling and obedience improving exercise but it is slightly more advanced in that the forehand, being off the track and without the guidance of the wall, may be more difficult to control.

When teaching this movement the easiest approach is from the half-pirouette in walk (Fig. 31). The outside leg creates the position, the inside leg maintains the impulsion and helps maintain the bend which is asked for with the inside hand. The outside hand controls the bend and the speed.

On completion of the *renvers* the forehand must be taken back on to the track and the horse ridden forward with impulsion.

The rein back
The following definition of the *rein back* is taken from the dressage rules and the rather quaint English is the result of a somewhat literal translation.

'The *rein back* is an equilateral, retrograde movement in which the feet are raised and set down almost simultaneously by diagonal pairs; each forefoot being raised and set down an instant before the diagonal hindfoot, so that, on hard ground, as a rule four separate beats are clearly audible. The feet should be well raised and the hind feet remain well in line.

At the preceding halt, as well as during the *rein back*, the horse, although standing motionless and moving backwards respectively, remains 'on the bit', maintaining his desire to move forward.

Anticipation or precipitation of the movement, resistance to or evasion of the hand, deviation of the quarters from the straight line, spreading or inactive hindlegs and dragging fore feet are serious faults.

If in a dressage test a trot or canter is required after a *rein back*, the horse should move off immediately into this pace, without a halt or an intermediate step.'

For *rein back* to comply with the demands of the dressage rules a supple, well balanced and obedient horse is required. The stepping backwards that one sees out hunting or on the polo ground is for practical purposes only and is usually not *rein back*. Under these circumstances the horse is asked to step backwards by the rider's hand and he probably does not step back in two time or straight; he probably also halts, having finished stepping back. All these actions would constitute serious faults in the *rein back* when performed in a dressage test.

From the very start the instructor must instil in his pupil that *rein back* is not made by pulling on the reins. It should be made from a square, well balanced halt with the horse on the bit showing no signs of resistance. The rider is asked to close his legs against the horse's sides as if he were about to walk forwards, but instead of allowing the horse to walk forwards he closes his fingers in a 'non-allowing' way which encourages the horse to step backwards. He must only step back the predetermined number of steps and then immediately step forwards, at whatever pace has been decided, without halting.

Where difficulty is experienced with this exercise the trainer can assist by tapping the horse lightly on the knee or fore arm with the whip as the rider applies the aids. Above all the rider must not be allowed to pull.

Simple change of leg at canter
This is a change of leg where the horse is brought back into walk and, after two or at the most three steps, is re-started into a canter with the other leg leading.

The *simple change* of leg at canter is yet another useful exercise for both the trainee horse and rider. For the horse it helps to improve his balance, his responsiveness to the aids and consequently his obedience. For the rider it helps to develop the subtle application of the aids and is a good exercise for establishing in the rider's mind the importance of the correct blend of seat, leg and hand in downward transitions. The *simple change* is best made across the diagonal of the school from a short, light canter with the rider asking the horse to walk at 'X', and having made three or four steps in walk, to strike off in canter on the new leading leg whilst still on the diagonal line.

In the downward transition the trainer must insist that the minimum amount of hand is used. The rider should sink softly down into the saddle, maintaining contact with the legs and using the fingers of the outside hand to apply a 'give and take' aid on the rein. It is important that the leg contact should be maintained to keep impulsion in the few steps in walk as otherwise the strike off into the new canter will be difficult and incorrect.

The aids for walk to canter are the same as those used for trot to canter. The novice rider will often feel that he has to make stronger aids or use greater effort from walk to canter than from trot to canter. This is not so and should not be necessary if the quality of the walk is sufficiently good for the horse to strike off into canter with ease.

Counter canter

This is a movement when the rider on a circle to the left deliberately makes his horse canter with the right canter lead (with the off-fore leading). The *counter canter* is a suppling movement. The horse maintains his natural flexion at the poll to the outside of the circle, and is therefore bent to the side of the leading leg. His conformation does not permit his spine to be bent to the line of the circle. The rider should especially endeavour to limit the deviation of the quarters to the outside of the circle, and restrict his demands according to the degree of suppleness of the horse. This is a particularly good suppling exercise for the horse and helps to develop his obedience, and for the rider is a good lesson in 'feel'. *Counter canter* can be made in working canter on large circles and bends. The circle can only be made smaller as the canter becomes more collected. *Counter canter* is of no value if the horse is sloppy or off the bit.

Ideally the rider should ride in *counter canter* exactly as he would in canter but in fact it may be necessary, on some horses, to maintain the correct bend by the use of the inside hand and leg and to carry the outside leg a little behind the girth almost towards the canter aid.

(*opposite*) The half-pass to the right (explained on the next page) (*By courtesy of the British Horse Society*)

The trainer must take care that the quarters are not allowed to swing either in or out on the circle. The *counter canter* lesson can be started off by making small loops off the long side of the school and returning to the track taking care to maintain the correct bend in the horse. When making this preparatory work there is a danger that the hind feet will not follow in the line of tracks made by the fore feet and that the horse will make a sort of half-pass off the track and leg yield back on to the track.

These loops can be made deeper until the horse can be ridden from quarter marker to quarter marker and remain in balanced *counter canter* through the corner and round the end of the school.

Half-pass
This is described in the rules of the International Equestrian Federation as follows:

> '*Half-pass.* This is a variation of travers, executed 'on the diagonal' instead of 'along the wall'. The horse slightly bent round the inside leg of the rider should be as close as possible parallel to the long sides of the arena, although the forehand should be slightly in advance of the quarters. The outside legs pass and cross in front of the inside legs. The horse is looking in the direction in which he is moving. He should maintain the same rhythm and balance throughout the whole movement.
>
> In order to give more freedom and mobility to the shoulders, which adds to the ease and grace of the movement, it is of great importance, not only that the horse is correctly bent and thereby prevented from protruding his inside shoulder, but also to maintain the impulsion, especially the engagement of the inside hindleg.'

If the preparatory work has been diligently carried out and the horse is supple, responsive to the aids and capable of working with a degree of collection, the *half-pass* should come fluently and correctly. If however the preparatory work has been incorrect, various difficulties may be encountered, such as: the quarters leading; insufficient or incorrect bend; insufficient collection, and a lack of impulsion.

A successful way to start this work is to make a 10m circle in collected trot in the corner of the school to establish the correct bend. On completion of the circle the rider is asked to ride down the centre line for a few steps and then to draw back the outside leg to apply the quarter controlling aid, asking the

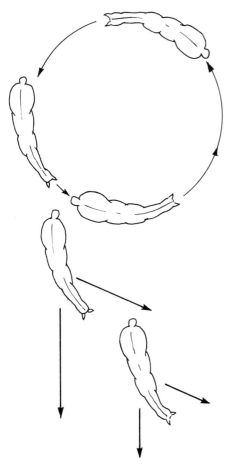

Fig 32 The half-pass from a
10m circle

quarters to move away from the leg. The inside hand asks for
the bend, the outside hand controls the bend and the speed and
the inside leg at the girth maintains the impulsion which is so
important for the correct execution of this exercise (Fig. 32).

The trainer must pay particular attention to the basic faults
which often occur in this exercise:

a) The rider unbalanced, with weight usually to the outside.
b) The quarters leading, sometimes due to excessive or
incorrect use of the outside leg. This is also sometimes caused
by use of the leg yielding exercise in the same way.
c) Insufficient bend in the horse.
d) Loss of impulsion due to the rider neglecting to maintain the
correct control with the inside leg.

Flying change of leg at canter

This change of leg is executed in close connection with the suspension which follows each stride of the canter. *Flying changes* of leg can also be executed in series, for instance at every stride, or at every second, third or fourth stride. The horse remains light, calm and straight with lively impulsion, maintaining the same rhythm and balance throughout the series concerned. In order not to restrict or restrain the lightness and fluency of the *flying changes* of leg in series, the degree of collection should be slightly less than usual at collected canter.

The *flying change* is probably the most exciting and satisfying exercise in equitation; it demands immense dexterity and understanding from the horse and great feel and co-ordination from the rider. Before any rider is encouraged to teach his horse the *flying change* he must have been trained, in this exercise, on a horse that makes correct changes in response to correct aids. This is essential if the rider is to have any good effect on his own untrained horse.

There are a number of ways in which both horse and rider can be introduced to making the *flying change*. It is recommended that the instructor should thoroughly understand and be practised in each method. Whilst he may find one which is generally more advantageous, occasions will arise where one of the other methods may suit a particular horse or rider. A complete understanding of the various methods with their advantages and disadvantages will put the instructor in a much stronger position to defend the one which he chooses to use.

Before *flying change* is attempted the trainer must ensure that the horse which his pupil is riding is capable of making the walk to canter and canter to walk transitions with balance and calmness. He must be able to perform these on both reins in the corners, going straight on the track and down the centre line. He must also be able to strike off in counter canter from walk on the track, going straight down the centre line and in the corners. Both rider and horse have a fair chance of achieving *flying changes* providing they are capable of these transitions, and the canter itself must have a degree of collection and be light and calm.

Flying change can be taught by changing the rein in canter from quarter marker to quarter marker and making the change from counter canter tò true canter in the next corner. It can be made from a half circle in canter off the track and by making the change as the track is met on the new rein, or it can be made from counter canter on the large circle.

This first method, by changing the rein in canter across the diagonal, should be executed as follows. The lesson should, as always, start with ten or fifteen minutes of warming up exercises for both horse and rider. After this initial period, and whilst the horse is still fresh, the student should work on the canter to walk and walk to canter transitions starting in the corner and then straight on the track, followed by transitions down the centre line. Once these are established at a satisfactory standard the walk to *counter canter* transitions can be practised, starting straight down the centre line, followed by straight on the track and finally in the corners. If these have all been successful, then both horse and rider should be in a good position to attempt *flying change*.

The trainer must decide on which rein the horse prefers to canter, as this is the rein to which we are going to attempt to change. For the purpose of this lesson we will assume that the horse prefers to canter to the left. We put him into canter right, make half a circuit of the school and change the rein, say, from 'K' to 'M'. As the student crosses the 'X' marker he is asked to 'forget that you are in canter, think of yourself as being in sitting trot, and in the corner after "M" canter left'. If the preparatory work has been correct and the student applies the aids correctly the horse will make the *flying change*.

This may seem an oversimplification, but it has several distinct advantages:

a) It discourages the student rider from making too much preparation.

b) Until the rider becomes really quite advanced he will find it difficult to try to co-ordinate the application of the canter leg aids with the footfalls of the horse, so to think of making the *flying change* as making canter from trot may be helpful.

c) It may help the rider as the horse is mechanically encouraged to change in the corner from counter canter on the leg that he finds least comfortable to canter on the leg which he finds easier.

The disadvantages of making *flying change* in this way are:

a) The horse may learn to anticipate the change and disobediently change each time he enters a corner in counter canter. This often results in the horse changing only in front which can be a very troublesome problem.

b) It involves both horse and rider in a double task of riding the corner correctly and the problems of making the change.

In the second method, the rider makes a 15m circle in canter off the track from the half marker, and a smooth angle back to the track to change leg as the horse reaches it on his new rein. It is based on the principle that the horse will want to change from counter canter on the leading leg that he enjoys least to ordinary canter on the leading leg that he enjoys most. The preparatory work and warming up should be the same as for the first method.

Having made two or three complete 15m circles from the half marker in canter on the rein that the horse least enjoys, the rider is then asked to make a half circle and a smooth angle back to the track to join it before reaching the quarter marker. He should be asked to walk as he reaches the track and after two or three steps to strike off in canter on his new rein. Having made this simple change on rejoining the track two or three times, he can then be told again to think that he is in sitting trot as he makes his angle back to the track, and as he reaches it to apply the aids to canter on his new rein, so making the *flying change*. The disadvantage of this method is that, once again, the *flying change* is involved with a change of direction which may lead to problems when making a series of tempo changes which must be on a straight line.

The third method may be considered to be, classically, the most correct. Here the rider is asked to work on a large circle to the left or to the right. He makes frequent transitions from walk to canter and canter to walk, remaining on the large circle and making the strike off both to the left and to the right. The number of steps in both walk and canter should be varied, as should the direction of the strike off.

Having established good quality walk to canter and canter to walk transitions on the circle, the number of steps in walk can be reduced until the horse is making *flying change* in response to the canter aids from right to left or from left to right. Once again success in this exercise is more likely if the horse is asked to change from counter canter to canter on the rein which he finds easier.

The advantage of this method is that the horse is being asked to change his canter lead entirely by the correct use of the aids and there is no reliance on either the change of direction or the horse feeling that here is a logical place to change the lead both of which introduce an element of disobedience. An added advantage is that both rider and trainer have an unlimited number of opportunities to ask for the change. This enables the rider to give the aid when he feels that the horse is ready, rather than at any particular part of the school. The instructor must be very careful not to go on with this exercise for too long, particularly if tension and anticipation is building up in the horse.

If both horse and rider are new to this work, the easier change must be worked on until it can be performed confidently and calmly. The change in the opposite direction can then be introduced.

Where the horse is making this work for the first time he must be adequately rewarded after one change, and the rider should dismount and finish for that day. This work is physically demanding on the horse and should not be continued for more than three or four days before different work is introduced for variety.

Pirouettes
a) The *pirouette (half-pirouette)* is a circle (half-circle), executed on two tracks, with a radius equal to the length of the horse, and the forehand moving round the haunches.

b) *Pirouettes (half-pirouettes)* are usually carried out at collected walk or canter, but can also be executed at piaffer.

c) At the *pirouette (half-pirouette)* the fore feet and the outside hind foot move round the inside hind foot, which forms the pivot and should return to the same spot, or slightly in front of it, each time it leaves the ground.

d) At whatever pace the *pirouettes (half-pirouettes)* are executed, the horse, slightly bent to the direction in which he is turning, should remain 'on the bit' with a light contact and turn smoothly round, maintaining the exact rhythm and sequence of footfalls in that pace.

Fig 33 The quarter-pirouette

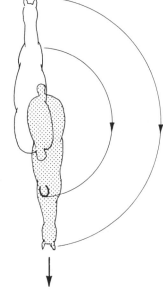

Fig 34 The half-pirouette

e) During the *pirouettes (half-pirouettes)* the horse should maintain his impulsion, and never move backwards or deviate sideways. If the inside hind foot is not raised and returned to the ground in the same rhythm as the outside hind foot, the pace is no longer regular.

f) The quality of the *pirouettes (half-pirouettes)* is judged according to the suppleness, lightness, cadence and regularity of the movement, and to the precision and smoothness of the transitions; *pirouettes (half-pirouettes)* at canter are also judged according to the balance, the elevation and the number of strides used. Ideally a *pirouette* should be executed in 6–8 strides, and a *half-pirouette* in 3–4 strides.

The half-pirouette in walk. Ulla Peterson of Sweden on Chigwell (*Findlay Davidson*)

The walk pirouette The *pirouette* in walk is a turn on the haunches in which the horse pivots around his inside hind foot whilst maintaining the regular, even, four-time tempo of his walk. Any loss of this tempo is a serious fault.

The *pirouette* is made in collected walk and is best introduced to both horse and rider by making a 6m volte in walk. The aids for making this volte are exactly the same as the aids for making any other circle. As the horse improves in making the volte the size can be decreased until the horse can

The canter pirouette. Harry Boldt of West Germany on Woyceck (*Findlay Davidson*)

(*opposite*) The canter pirouette to the right. Gabrielle Grillot of West Germany on Ultimo (*Findlay Davidson*)

make the first quarter of the volte into a *quarter-pirouette* (Fig. 33). This is achieved by the rider slightly varying the blend of the volte aids. The inside hand now has to invite the horse round on a shorter route, the outside hand prevents him from walking forwards on the circle, the outside leg acts as the quarter controlling leg and asks the quarters to come round, whilst the inside leg remains at the girth to maintain the impulsion and to prevent the horse from stepping backwards.

Having completed the *quarter-pirouette* the horse should be ridden energetically forward in walk. Once the *quarter-pirouette* has been mastered successfully the pupil can then go on to making a *half-pirouette* by continuing to apply the same aids (Fig. 34).

The canter pirouette This is a very advanced exercise and must not be attempted until the horse can work quietly and calmly in canter with a very high degree of collection. He must be able, whilst maintaining the clear three-time rhythm, to slow the canter steps right down until he is almost cantering on the spot, but keeping good impulsion.

There are a number of important factors to bear in mind when teaching this exercise:

a) The rider *must* maintain a correct, upright, balanced position.
b) The work is very tiring on the horse and should not be over-done.
c) The *full pirouette* should be built up through the quarter, the half and the three-quarter *pirouette.*
d) It is a great advantage if the rider can be trained first on a horse that will perform this exercise well when the correct aids are applied.

As in all advanced work this exercise can be introduced to the horse and rider in a number of ways. It is for the trainer to decide which of these approaches is best for a particular pupil.

a) Whilst making a large *pirouette* in walk the horse can be asked to strike off in canter, make two or three steps in *canter pirouette* and then be sent straight forwards in canter. If the balance is lost or the work deteriorates the horse should be returned to walk and sent straight forwards. The walk to

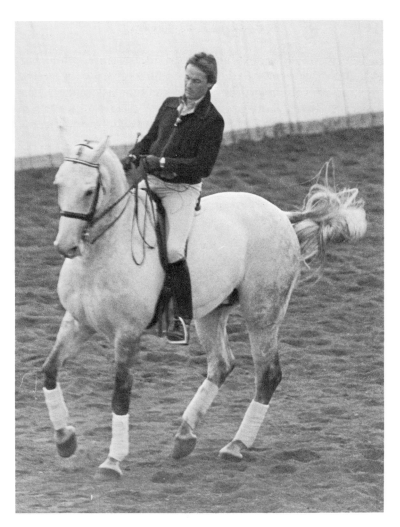

Working up to the canter pirouette. David Hunt of Great Britain on Marco Polo (*Author*)

canter strike off must be of high quality if this method is to be successful.

b) A small half circle of about 6m is made in collected canter at the end of the long side of the school. The horse is then ridden down the long side in renvers and the *half-pirouette* is made towards the wall. This method is particularly useful if the hind quarters have been swinging out in previous attempts which is a frequent difficulty in this exercise.

c) It is sometimes helpful to make a few steps in *canter pirouette* from a good half-pass as the bend should be correct, the collection good and the outside hind leg well engaged.

d) The *canter pirouette* can be made eventually on a straight line, when a degree of success has been achieved with one or more of the previous methods. Just before the point at which the *pirouette* or *half-pirouette* is to be made the horse should be put into a degree of shoulder-in to correct the bend, control the shoulders, and help achieve sufficient collection.

Piaffer

The *piaffer* is a highly measured, collected, elevated and cadenced trot on the spot. The horse's back is supple and vibrating. The quarters are slightly lowered, the haunches with active hocks are well engaged giving great freedom, lightness and mobility to the shoulders and forehand. Each diagonally opposed pair of feet is raised and returned to the ground alternately, with an even rhythm and a slightly prolonged suspension.

In principle, the height of the toe of the raised foreleg should be level with the middle of the canon bone of the other foreleg. The toe of the raised hindleg should reach just above the fetlock joint of the other hindleg.

Teaching the *piaffer* to horse and rider is a task for the experienced trainer only. The exercise is the culmination of maximum impulsion and lightness of the forehand. When the horse is capable of a high degree of collection and can make the transitions from collected trot to halt and collected trot to working trot smoothly, combined with the ability to make collected walk whilst remaining straight and calm, *piaffer* can be attempted.

It should first be made in hand with the horse dressed as for lungeing with the side reins sufficiently short to prevent him bending his neck too much to the left or the right when in his collected outline. This training is best carried out to start with on the track with the horse parallel to the wall.

When working on the left rein the trainer holds the lunge rein with his left hand and a long whip (not a lungeing whip) in his right hand. The horse is worked in collected walk and the speed gradually reduced by the use of the lunge rein which is held up fairly close to the lunge cavesson. The impulsion is

The piaffer. Harry Boldt of West Germany on Woyceck (*Findlay Davidson*)

maintained by the trainer tapping the horse lightly below the hocks with the long whip. As soon as one or two steps are made in *piaffer*, whilst still moving slightly forwards, the horse is allowed to go forwards and is rewarded by a pat on the neck. The exercise should be made with frequent changes of rein.

Once the *piaffer* is becoming established in hand, it can be attempted with the rider in the saddle. The work is once again made from collected walk, the rider slowing down the speed with the fingers and maintaining the impulsion with his seat and legs. The trainer may still help from the ground by tapping the hindlegs alternately just below the hocks in rhythm with the steps. It is very important at this stage that the horse is allowed to go forwards a little as he makes *piaffer*. Only in the most advanced tests is *piaffer* required on the spot. It is always better if the horse is going forward a little; he must never step back.

Passage

This is a measured, very collected, very elevated and very cadenced trot. It is characterised by a pronounced engagement of the quarters, a more accentuated flexion of the knees and hocks, and a graceful elasticity of movement. Each diagonally opposed pair of feet is raised and returned to the ground alternately, with an even rhythm and a prolonged suspension. In principle the height of the toe of the raised foreleg should be level with the middle of the canon bone of the other foreleg.

The passage. Harry Boldt of West Germany on Sando Kahn (*Findlay Davidson*)

The toe of the raised hindleg should be slightly above the fetlock joint of the other hindleg.

The neck should be raised and gracefully arched with the poll as the highest point and the head close to the perpendicular. The horse should remain light and 'on the bit' and should go smoothly from the *passage* to the piaffer and vice versa, with no apparent effort and without altering the rhythm. The impulsion should always be lively and pronounced.

Irregular steps with the hindlegs and swinging the forehand or the quarters from one side to the other are both serious faults.

This is a very advanced exercise and is probably the ultimate test of the rider's 'feel' and the correct logical training of his horse. If the horse is working well in piaffer and is willing to go freely forwards from it the rider should not find a few steps in *passage* too difficult. The horse is sent energetically forwards from piaffer by the rider's seat and legs, with the hands allowing him to go forwards but at the same time restraining the movement sufficiently to produce the graceful elevated steps of *passage*.

It must be remembered that *passage* requires great physical effort from the horse and only a few steps should be asked for at first. On completion of the few steps in *passage* the horse should be ridden forwards in collected trot to ensure that this does not deteriorate as a result of the introduction of *passage*.

Other Schooling Exercises not included in the Dressage Test

Turn on the forehand
This is a controversial exercise used by some trainers to improve the horse's co-ordination and to encourage him to move away from the rider's leg. It is often used as a fundamental introduction to lateral work. It can be made in two ways, firstly with the horse looking away from the direction in which he is turning and secondly, with the horse looking towards the way he is turning. *Turn on the forehand* is made from the halt which encourages those who are opposed to it to say that it is an exercise made without impulsion, and which therefore puts unnecessary strain on the fetlock joints of the forelegs.

To perform the exercise correctly the horse is brought to the halt on the inside track, standing square and on the bit. If the horse is to turn to the right he is bent a little in that direction with the right hand. The right leg drawn back behind the girth then asks the horse to move his hindquarters round with regular, even steps. The left hand prevents the horse from moving forwards and the left leg is kept in contact to prevent him from stepping back (Fig. 35). The aids for a *turn on the forehand* to the left are the reverse of those used for a turn to the right. On completion of the turn the horse should be ridden forwards with impulsion. As the horse pivots around the inside fore foot in this exercise, it should be used in moderation to avoid putting too great a strain on the fetlock joint. A further disadvantage is that it may encourage the horse to come on to his forehand.

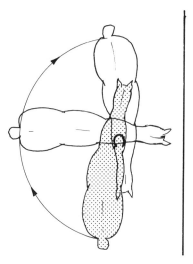

Fig 35 The turn on the forehand to the right

There is a similar exercise, sometimes called the *turn about the forehand*, in which the horse walks a small circle with his fore feet and a larger circle with his hind feet to make a 180° turn. This is somewhat more acceptable in that it can be made with impulsion and the four-time tempo of the walk can be maintained.

The half-halt! (*Findlay Davidson*)

The half-halt
This exercise entails re-balancing the horse before attempting a transition or a movement. It consists of checking the speed of the horse with the fingers of the outside hand whilst maintaining the impulsion with the inside leg or the leg and the seat. It is an important exercise which should be taught to all riders, and its importance should be thoroughly understood by those who train competition riders.

6
Teaching
the Rider to Jump

Jumping technique, as we know it today, is a direct result of the thoughts and work of Captain Federico Caprilli who was the Riding Master at the Italian Cavalry School at the turn of the century. Before that time it was usual for the rider to lean back when jumping, therefore preventing the horse from using himself to the best of his ability. Caprilli saw how vital it was for the horse to have the full use of his head, neck and back to be able to jump and go fast across country. He therefore devised a style of riding in which the rider leaned forwards to take the weight directly off the horse's back and moved his hands forwards to allow the horse to balance himself. Whilst Caprilli personally did not incline the top part of his body as far forwards as riders do today, he was the instigator of what was to become known as the 'forward seat'.

The principles for jumping are exactly the same as they are for riding on the flat; the horse must go forwards, calmly and straight and the rider must be balanced, still and correct in his riding position.

When jumping, the rider is asked to shorten his stirrups two or three holes from his flat work length. This enables him to incline the top part of his body forwards which he needs to do to stay in balance with his horse. When deciding how much to shorten the stirrups it is a good guide to fit the rider's knee correctly into the knee roll of the jumping saddle. If the saddle

(*opposite above*) The horse and rider in perfect balance. Lucinda Prior-Palmer of Great Britain on Killaire at the Dog Kennels at Badminton, 1980 (*Findlay Davidson*)

(*opposite below*) Joaquin Perez de las Heras of Mexico on Alymony in the Nations Cup at Aachen, 1980 (*Findlay Davidson*)

is the correct size for the rider this should give him the correct length of stirrup leather. The instructor must also take into account the rider's length of leg, and must use his discretion to assess the correct length for each pupil.

Once again it is very much to the rider's advantage if he can start his jumping on a 'schoolmaster' horse before he attempts to jump a young or untrained horse. Learning on an experienced horse that will approach the fence calmly and well balanced, taking regular, even strides will give the pupil confidence and will help towards achieving the correct mental and physical approach.

Before the pupil is introduced to jumping he must have an independent seat. This entails being able to walk, trot and canter on a trained horse maintaining his balance by a correct yet supple position therefore leaving his legs and hands free to apply the aids. He should also have been trained in all three paces over undulating country and be able to ride confidently at each without stirrups.

The training should start with the pupil trotting over poles on the ground, placed about 137cm apart for a 16 hand horse. Three or five poles are better than two, four or six poles, as the horse is less likely to attempt to jump poles two at a time if there is an odd number. The rider is asked to trot through the poles at working rising trot, maintaining the correct tempo and speed. When he has established this and can remain in balance throughout, a jump or cavaletti at about 34–5cm high can be introduced 3m from the last trotting pole (Fig. 36). The rider is then asked to come through the trotting poles again and over the small jump, making sure that he stays inclined a little bit forwards from the hips, he keeps his leg still and in the correct position, and he looks straight ahead and maintains a sure, but 'allowing', rein contact.

It is sometimes an advantage to fit a neck strap to the horse so that the rider can hold it if he feels he is going to be left behind when the horse jumps. If however the horse is suitable and the rider has achieved the standard of riding described earlier in this chapter, the neck strap should not be necessary.

(*opposite*) Former Dutch junior international, now riding for West Germany, Franke Sloothank on the veteran Rex-the-Robber at Aachen, 1980 (*Findlay Davidson*)

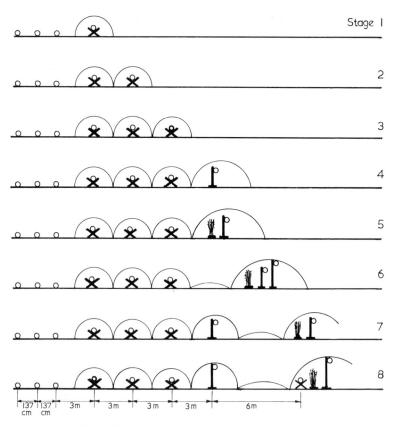

2

3

4

5

6

7

8

137 137 3m 3m 3m 3m 6m
cm cm

Fig 36 The build up of progressive gymnastic jumping exercises

Once the pupil has successfully negotiated the trotting poles and one cavaletti, a second cavaletti can be added 6m from the first. The pupil will then have to trot through the poles, jump the first cavaletti, take one stride in canter and jump the second cavaletti.

The object of this type of jumping training is to build up the rider's agility and confidence progressively until he can go forwards in balance with his horse on the approach to the jump, on take-off, over the jump and on landing. Throughout these exercises the rider must be encouraged to sit still, maintaining a sure, steady, even rein contact and with a still, quiet leg. He must be ready at any stage to apply the aids with the legs and seat or hands as required.

The exercise can be continued by increasing the number of cavaletti after the trotting poles and varying the distance between them so that the horse takes one canter stride between them or jumps straight in and out with no canter stride. This variation in the exercise improves the co-ordination, agility and confidence of both horse and rider.

The next stage is to replace the last cavaletti by a small spread fence about 50cm in height. Once the rider's position has been established over the line of cavaletti in canter he should be able to negotiate the small fence on the end without spoiling his position, rein or leg contact. There is a danger here in that the rider, particularly if he has some previous jumping experience, may feel that he must make some special effort over the last jump and kick hard with his legs, drive with his seat, flap his elbows, make an exaggerated dive forwards with the upper part of his body or a combination of any of these activities which, of course, frustrates the whole object of this system of jumping training. He must therefore be warned that no extra effort is required over the last jump and that the whole purpose of the exercise is that he should establish his still, quiet position over the trotting poles and cavaletti and maintain it over the last jump.

Heinrich-Wilhelm Johannsmann of West Germany on Excellenz at Aachen, 1980 (*Findlay Davidson*)

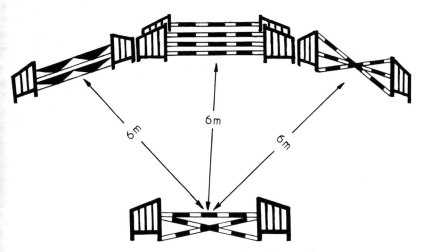

Fig 37 The layout of various jumping exercises

The exercise can be made more demanding by replacing the cavaletti with small, varied jumps. Crossed poles, a small brush or wall, a staircase or spread fence will add variety and introduce the rider to the types of obstacle that he will have to jump singly later (Fig. 37). The fences used must always be inviting and the distances between them correct. Nothing must ever be introduced that discourages the horse from going freely forwards in a good rhythm.

Once the rider can negotiate a line of trotting poles and cavaletti or small jumps he can attempt to negotiate a small single fence from canter. The siting of the fence and its construction should be carefully considered. The fence should preferably be placed alongside the riding school wall or another fence to encourage the horse to go straight on the approach. To assist the horse to approach the fence on a good stride it should be built carefully on the track so that the rider, having ridden a correct corner of the school or manege, will reach the jump on an accurate stride. Assuming that the rider makes a quarter of a 15m circle at canter through the corner, the jump should be about 22.5m from the corner to allow the horse to take five canter strides before reaching the jump. To

(*opposite*) John Whitaker of Great Britain on Ryan's Son, winner of the second qualifier for the German International Championship at Aachen, 1980 (*Findlay Davidson*) make absolutely certain of the strides approaching and including take-off, a pole can be placed on the ground 3m in front of the jump to help both horse and rider to see and feel the point of take-off. The jump itself should be inviting with substantial wings, for example a small brush at about 60cm with a pole above it at about 75cm and a second pole to produce a spread of about 60cm.

The rider should be told to approach the fence in exactly the same way as he rode down the line of cavaletti, sitting still, maintaining his position, feeling the rhythm of the horse's stride, keeping a definite contact with his legs and a sure but 'allowing' contact with his hands.

(*opposite above*) Gert Wiltfang of West Germany on Roman, the individual gold medallist in the European Show Jumping Championships in Rotterdam, 1979 (*Findlay Davidson*)

(*opposite below*) The strength and balance of the Italian seat. Captain Raimondo d'Inzeo of Italy on Belle Vue (*Findlay Davidson*)

(*below*) Liz Edgar of Great Britain on Forever in the Nations Cup at Hickstead, 1980, looking for the next fence (*Findlay Davidson*)

There is a variation to this style in which the rider, with a rather longer stirrup leather, approaches the fence in an upright position and is very quick to get forward on take-off and is rather more upright as the horse lands. This style has been developed for very competent riders, riding strong, fit horses with well established, round outlines. It is particularly effective over very big fences in a small, indoor arena where maximum control and balance are required. This technique is a refinement of the basic jumping technique and should not be introduced to the novice jumping rider until he has mastered and is experienced in the more elementary style of jumping.

There is no doubt that whilst both riders and horses must train over jumps and courses similar to those that they are likely to meet in competition, their gymnastic jumping training is a most important part of their preparation. A number of these exercises can be prepared before the lesson begins so that both horse and rider, having warmed up, can go straight on without a long delay whilst jumps are erected.

The two following groups of exercises have proved both useful and convenient.

In the first, the equipment is set out as in Figure 38. There are three trotting poles 137cm apart and a gap of 3m before the first jump which is a single pole at about 61cm. Jumps 2 and 3 are more single poles about 1m apart or with enough room for a horse to pass between the inside wing stands. The fourth jump is an oxer type fence about 76cm high with a 76cm spread, with the back pole one hole higher than the front pole.

The first exercise is for the rider to approach in trot through the trotting poles, jump fence number 1, make three strides in canter, pass between jumps 2 and 3 and jump fence number 4. The emphasis should be on correct riding throughout with the horse going forwards straight and calmly with good rhythm and balance. In the second exercise the rider approaches on the right rein, through the trotting poles, over fence number 1, makes one stride in canter and jumps fence number 2. In the third exercise the rider approaches on the left rein, trots through the trotting poles, jumps fence number 1, makes one stride in canter and jumps fence number 3.

(*opposite*) A polished, well-balanced team. Carlos Delia of the Argentine on Cardon (*Findlay Davidson*)

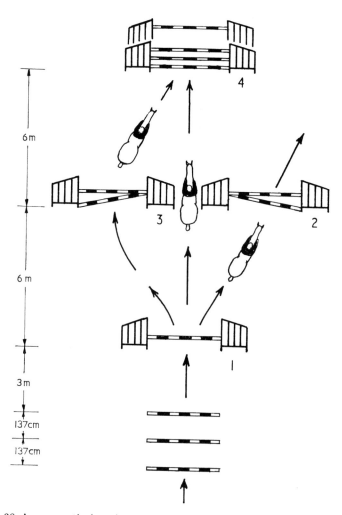

Fig 38 A gymnastic jumping exercise involving a one-stride double and changes of direction

The trainer must pay particular attention to the quality of the work between exercises. Having jumped fences 1 or 2 the rider must quickly but calmly and correctly return to trot to resume the exercise. He must not be allowed to be slack or careless between exercises.

Exercises 4 and 5 take exercises 2 and 3 a stage further in that the rider is asked to go left after fence 2 or right after fence 3, take one stride in canter and jump fence 4. It must be made quite clear to the rider that he must only go on to fence 4

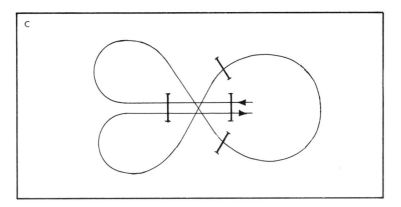

Fig 39 Gymnastic jumping exercises involving a change of rein to the right or to the left

if he is in control and can jump the fence in a calm and balanced way. If it is going to involve a struggle in any way he must ride away and re-establish his control and balance before attempting to jump.

In the second group of exercises the jumps can be set up before the lesson starts, leaving the track free for warming up and other preparatory exercises. Figure 39 shows the layout of the fences. There are of course many types that can be utilised but it should be remembered that all the fences must be built to be jumped in both directions, and a selection of tracks should be ridden to give this exercise variety (Figs. 39 a, b, c).

Whilst the instructor must pay attention to the actual jumping in this exercise, it is particularly useful for training students to ride correctly between fences maintaining their balance, bend, control, calmness and impulsion. It teaches the pupil to use the arena correctly and to full advantage and to plan ahead.

Further training to improve the jumping rider
Having established a degree of confidence and competence in the rider which enables him to jump a course of small fences up to 1m high, the trainer must then go on to teach him:

a) How to walk a course, either in show jumping or cross country.
b) How to ride a course of jumps at a required speed.
c) How to cope with jumps of different types.

Further training must then include gymnastic work that will improve his confidence, agility, balance, grip and fitness, all of which will be needed at some stage in the 'rough and tumble' of competition riding.

Walking the jumping course
Training here must include:

a) Reading the schedule and knowing the conditions of the competition, such as the speed and the table under which it is being held.

(*opposite*) A balanced horse and rider on a steep slope (*Clive Hiles*)

b) Studying the course plan, taking particular note of the location of the start and finish and any obligatoirs through which the rider must pass.

c) Allowing enough time to walk the course without being rushed. It may be necessary on occasions to walk it a second or third time.

d) Careful study of the line that the rider intends to take, paying particular attention to where he can take short cuts, the stretches on which he may be able to make up time and those where he must go slowly.

e) The way the rider intends to jump each individual fence with special attention as to what he will do where there is a choice of routes. Here he should consider what to do in the event of a refusal at his first choice, as it may be sensible to take an easier route than to risk a second refusal.

f) The measurement of the distances between combination fences. He must learn to pace out the distance between fences so that he knows exactly how many strides his horse will take between them and how he will have to influence these strides.

Christopher Bealby of Great Britain on Jack be Nimble on the steeplechase course at Badminton, 1979 (*Findlay Davidson*)

Hugh Thomas of Great Britain on Mythic Light over the ninth steeplechase fence at Badminton, 1980 (*Findlay Davidson*)

Riding a course at a required speed

A competition course invariably has to be ridden at a specified number of metres per minute, the pace being slower for novice competitions and faster for more advanced competitions.

It is important that the competition rider is trained to ride at the speed demanded by the rules. It is infuriating to incur unnecessary time faults but it is also wasteful to ride the horse too fast, particularly if there are further phases of the competition for which the horse will require maximum energy. Training to ride a show jumping course in the required time is largely a matter of practice and will improve with experience and knowledge of the horse's capabilities.

When riding the roads and tracks phases of a horse trial the rider must be trained to use his watch, paying particular attention to the kilometre markers en route. Some trainers and riders find it useful to write the check times, by kilometre markers, on a card which is taped to the rider's forearm. This enables the competitor to check whether he is up or down on his time schedule.

For the steeple chase phase the competitor must learn to gallop at 690m per minute. This is not particularly fast, but the trainer must find a way to help his rider to assess the correct speed avoiding time faults or taking too much out of his horse. Several racecourses have facilities for motor cars to be driven alongside outside the rail. If permission can be obtained to gallop on one of these from time to time it is very convenient for the trainer to drive alongside his galloping pupil setting the exact speed.

Riding the cross country phase at the correct speed is largely a matter of experience again, but when training at home some time must be spent on riding across varying terrain and jumping fences at the speed required under the supervision of the trainer with a stopwatch. An important point that appears to be overlooked by many trainers is that where riders are required to carry extra weights in competition to meet a minimum weight requirement, this weight (or at least some of it) should be carried in training. It is a serious mistake to leave the carrying of the extra weight until the day of the competition.

Coping with jumps of various types
The rider must be trained to vary his approach to particular fences in order to cope with the problems set by the different designs.

The steeple chase fence, which is thick and slopes away with a good ground line, is generally inviting and the horse can brush through the top 25cm or so. Therefore it can be approached on a good long stride at the gallop. On the other hand the stile which is narrow, upright and with no ground line or wings will require a more accurate approach and more precise jumping. These are the two extremes and there are many other types of fence and approach which need careful consideration. Jumping up and down hill, into and out of water, up and down banks and drops all need to be carefully studied. Combination fences often cause problems to both horse and rider. The jumping trainer must school his pupils over combination fences varying the number of strides between the elements, the number of elements in the combination and the design of each one. He must never set distances between fences which are incorrect or discourage the

Mark Todd of New Zealand on Southern Comfort on the advanced cross-country course at Rushall, 1980 (*Findlay Davidson*)

horse from attempting to jump the combination with confidence. A guide to recommended distances in combination fences is shown in Figures 40 a and b.

Gymnastic jumping training for the rider
Work without stirrups will improve the rider's balance and confidence. A certain amount of rising trot without stirrups will improve the rider's grip and strengthen and condition the leg muscles. This training should be watched very carefully by the instructor as, although it is very beneficial to the jumping rider, it may spoil his seat and position on the flat should he begin to grip up excessively.

Gymnastic jumping without stirrups down a lane of cavaletti or jumps, and later with the reins knotted and the rider's arms folded, will all help to build a confident, fit and agile competition rider.

A guide to recommended distances in combination jumping

(a) *Suitable distances for horses*

For combination obstacles the following average distances are suggested for horses according to the type of obstacles included in the combination

(b) *Suitable distances for ponies*
Suggested distances for 14.2hh ponies. It is suggested for
12.2hh and 13.2hh ponies that the distances below be
reduced by 15cm in a one stride combination and 30cm
in a two stride combination

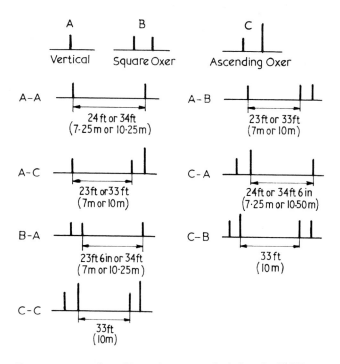

Because a pony's stride varies so much, it is safer NOT to
have a spread in the middle or at the end of a combination of a one stride distance

Fig 40 A guide to recommended distances in combination jumping: (a)
Suitable distances for horses; (b) Suitable distances for ponies (*Reproduced by
kind permission of the British Show Jumping Association*)

All competitors must learn to spring into the saddle from the
ground without the use of the stirrups. Valuable seconds are
often lost after a fall in a competition when the rider cannot
vault quickly into the saddle.

To compete successfully the rider must be physically fit. The
sight of a horse in a Three-Day Event or a Point-to-Point who
is fitter than his rider is not uncommon but is, of course, quite
unacceptable to the riding trainer. At the end of a hard race or
a testing cross country course a fit rider can be a considerable

A good upright schooling fence, well filled and inviting (*Author*)

A spread schooling fence, solid and attractive (*Author*)

help to his horse, whilst the unfit rider is a positive burden. It is the duty of the trainer therefore to ensure that both horse and rider are sufficiently fit to put into practice in competition everything that they have learned in training. Running or cycling and a few daily suppling exercises should be part of the daily programme of all competition riders be they concerned in eventing, show jumping, dressage or racing.

7

Classroom Teaching

Most riding instructors are at home in the riding school whether indoors or outside. This is the environment in which they have been trained and the workshop in which they pursue their chosen sport. The complete riding instructor must be able to teach not only in the riding school but in the classroom as well, but this is a prospect which fills most junior and some senior instructors with horror. This fear is quite unfounded as, by observing a few simple rules, classroom teaching can be a most rewarding and interesting challenge.

The following factors should therefore be considered when preparing a lesson:

The aim   The instructor must first define his aim. It must be clear, limited, simple and practicable. Before it can be considered practicable it must be related to:

The time   How long is the lesson?

The class   How many pupils are there?
How much do they know already?
How quickly can they learn?

Having decided on the aim the subject matter can now be considered.

Subject matter The instructor must know this thoroughly and must consider carefully the information required to achieve the aim. Having decided this it must be grouped under subject headings.

Ways of presentation Different ways will suggest themselves. The most suitable way for the subject must be selected.

Training aids The parts of the lesson which will require reinforcing with illustrations or training aids should be considered.

Conditions of work Is a classroom needed? Will the tack room or feed room do?

Successful instruction is based on the common sense and imaginative use of the following principles and techniques.

The principles Preparation and planning.
Promotion and the maintenance of the desire to learn.
Confirmation that instruction has been learned.
The techniques Question technique.
The use of training aids.

These principles and techniques should not be treated in isolation; they are closely related and should be combined to achieve the best results possible.

Preparation and Planning

Any lesson or lecture must be planned so that the various phases of instruction are presented logically and progressively. The lesson should be divided into three phases.

The beginning
Preliminaries Anything which cannot be done until the class assembles, such as giving out equipment, roll call, etc.

Revision Where there is a link with a previous lesson a short time should be spent on revision. This provides a good base on which to start the lesson and attunes the pupils' minds to the subject to be covered.

Introduction At this stage the instructor is able to introduce the subject and achieve the interest of his class by stating the aim clearly, and providing an incentive to learn where possible.

The middle
This part of the lesson contains the main teaching. The subject

matter must be divided into groups and the instructor must carefully eliminate anything which is either irrelevant or unnecessary. What remains must then be carefully arranged in logical order and at the end of each stage the instructor must confirm by question and answer technique that what he has taught has been absorbed by his class.

The end
To finish the lesson neatly the instructor should confirm that the class has understood what has been taught. This should be done by allowing questions from the class to enable them to clear up any doubts that may exist and by putting questions to the class or arranging a short test quiz.

Finally, he should sum up to emphasise the major points of the lesson, and should include a 'look forward' about the subject of the next lesson to arouse interest in it.

Promotion and maintenance of the desire to learn
As a rule people who come to an instructor to learn equitation and its related subjects do so because they have a real interest in the horse. For classroom instruction to be successful, however, interest in the subject must be stimulated.

Firstly, the class should be given something to look forward to in their next lesson. When running a course of instruction pupils should be given an interesting and attractively laid out written programme so that they know exactly what to expect at any particular period. Advertising the lesson can be of help; any display which will arouse curiosity will promote interest in the subject.

Once the lesson has started the introduction should include:
A clear statement of what is to be learned.
A realistic reason as to why this subject is important, and why it should be learned.
Whether or not there is any reward to be gained from knowledge of the subject.

The enthusiasm of the instructor will play a major part in maintaining the pupils' interest throughout the lesson. The good instructor will involve his pupils in as much activity as possible: mental activity when teaching facts and physical activity when teaching skills.

As many of the students' senses as possible should be involved. Hearing is most frequently involved in teaching, in that most instructors rely on speech to put their subjects across. Talking, however, can be monotonous and the dreary voice of many teachers has often sent the most enthusiastic student to sleep. The involvement of the class in touching, seeing, smelling and tasting, where applicable, will promote class activity and maintain lively interest. To give a simple example: it would be very difficult to teach a pupil to tie a bow-tie by just describing it to him verbally. It would be very much more effective to show him how it is done and then to give him a bow-tie to practise by himself under the instructor's guidance.

Instruction must be as realistic as possible. For instance, when teaching a pupil the principles of assessing the age of a horse by examination of the teeth, much can be done in the classroom, but the pupil must at some stage look into the mouth of a real horse to examine the teeth and complete this study.

Instruction must be related to everyday life and it is important that the instructor relates his teaching to practical situations that will be encountered by his pupils.

Interest can also be maintained by the use of clear and imaginative training aids such as films, slides, posters, the overhead projector, etc. These will be discussed later in this chapter.

Confirmation that instruction has been learned
The instructor must ensure that, as far as possible, the teaching has been absorbed and understood. The lesson must therefore develop in logical and limited stages towards the final aim, and the instructor should confirm that each stage has been thoroughly understood before he continues to the next.

At the end of the lesson both the instructor and the class will want to know how well they have done, which is best achieved by two-way questioning.

Question technique
To maintain class interest and to involve the pupils in the work the instructor must understand:

a) The purpose of questions in teaching.
b) How to put questions to the class.
c) How to answer questions from the class.

The purpose of questioning is threefold:

a) To teach, by making the class think out the answers by themselves.
b) To involve the class by keeping them mentally active.
c) To confirm that the lesson has been absorbed and understood.

When putting a question to the class it should be directed to the whole class, a pause made to allow each pupil time to think and then one pupil invited to answer. It is a mistake to nominate the student who is to answer before the question as this usually leads to the rest of the class breathing a sigh of relief and giving the matter no further thought.

The instructor should ensure that the question is understood and must avoid ambiguity. Questions which encourage guessing are of little value, and 50/50 questions come into this category. For instance, a question that requires an answer 'yes' or 'no' or 'black' or 'white' does not really test whether or not the lesson has been learned. Questions which test a skill or the pupils' powers of expression (unless of course this is the intention) should also be avoided.

When pupils are given the opportunity to question the instructor any question should be put back to the rest of the class. If the point has been generally missed it may show up a weakness in the instruction. If the question concerns a subject which is yet to be covered the class should be told that the matter will be dealt with at a later stage. Where the question reveals a deficiency in the lesson the instructor should take note and make the necessary corrections.

Irrelevant questions are often asked, and if the question is genuine it should be dealt with either by a brief answer or by explaining that it does not fit into that lesson and will be answered at another time. Above all this type of questioning should not be discouraged, but a deliberate 'red herring' must be squashed promptly and effectively.

When the question is relevant but the instructor does not know the answer, it is fatal for him to try to bluff his way out.

The instructor must admit that he does not know the answer and undertake to provide it at a later date, which obviously he must not then forget to do.

Good question technique stimulates class activity and keeps pupils alert. No one likes to look foolish but everyone enjoys answering correctly. A good question is one that the class can understand, is not ambiguous, discourages guessing and promotes thought.

Plan the questions and know the answers.

The use of training aids
Teaching can be made more clear and simple by the use of training aids. These are used to help the instructor by reinforcing his teaching.

Blackboard and chalk This equipment is cheap and simple and is available to most instructors. It is not, however, always used to the best advantage. White chalk is not always the clearest colour; yellow is often better and whilst red, blue and brown can make an interesting change and add variety, they are often difficult to see. Light shining on a blackboard can make it impossible for some of the class to see what is written.

Writing free hand on a blackboard requires practice and a little artistic flair. It is good preparation for the instructor to write on the blackboard in pencil before the class begins. The class cannot see what is written, but the instructor, standing close to the board, can see it clearly. This has several advantages: it provides him with an aide memoire, plans his writing on the blackboard, avoiding the embarrassment of running out of space, and prevents writing at an angle, mis-spelling or cramping an illustration.

Where a blackboard is to be prepared, the work will be much clearer if the chalk is first dipped in water, and as the chalk on the board dries it will become very bright and clear. If the work on the blackboard is to be kept, the chalk can be dipped into a solution of gum arabic which will result in the work drying up bright and semi-permanent.

Posters These can be easily and cheaply made. Chalk, felt tipped pen or poster paint are all useful mediums used on white or coloured paper. The advantage of the poster is that it can be easily rolled up and stored until required for display.

A useful training aid — the bone structure and X-section of the lower leg and hoof (*Author*)

Films and film strips Several are now available covering a wide range of subjects. It must be remembered, however, that the film will only support other teaching and should not be used in isolation. Where a film is used to present a subject on its own, the teacher must allow time for it to be discussed and for the pupils to ask questions. The disadvantage of films is that they require expensive projection equipment and a darkened room.

Slides These are cheap, easy to show and can be taken by an amateur photographer and used to illustrate a particular point. The apparatus required to show them is inexpensive and they can be easily arranged to illustrate a lesson quickly and effectively.

A portable overhead projector, very useful for the travelling instructor (*Author*)

The ultimate reward. Captain Mark Phillips, winner of the 1981 Badminton Horse Trials on Lincoln, receiving the Butler Challenge Bowl (awarded to the best British rider) from Her Majesty the Queen (*Jim Bennett*)

Models These are very useful where the real item is either unobtainable or inconvenient, for example the skeleton of the horse, a dressage arena or a show jumping course.

Specimens Very often the best way to demonstrate is to provide the student in the classroom with a specimen of the real thing, for example a surgical shoe, samples of oats or other cereals or the farrier's tools.

Actual equipment There are occasions on which it is possible to provide the actual equipment which is the subject of the lesson in the classroom. For example, when teaching the stripping and cleaning of clippers it is clearly an advantage to have the clippers in the class and to let the pupils individually handle them.

The overhead projector This is an expensive piece of equipment which will project a hand-made transparency on to a screen. The transparency can be easily made on a transparent sheet about one foot square by writing or drawing with a waxed crayon. This system gives considerable scope for building up a picture on the screen by laying one trasparency upon another. It is a most useful and convincing means of presentation.

Video recording This is a means of recording an activity on a cassette and being able to play it back through a normal television receiver. It is expensive but is particularly useful, as the pupils in the class can be recorded performing a particular task and later watch themselves on the screen with the obvious advantage of being able to discuss the results. A further advantage is that the tape can be stopped at any time to freeze a frame and can be rewound for a particular passage to be re-shown. A sound track can also be recorded on the video cassette.

The use of training aids must always be planned. They should be kept hidden until they are required and removed as soon as they are finished with, as they may otherwise cause distractions.

Remember that the aid is only to help the teacher to make his point; the teacher must teach, and the aid will emphasise certain aspects.

Classrooms Classrooms should be quiet and free from distractions. It is a mistake to have classroom walls covered with posters, no matter how attractive or interesting they are, as they cause distractions and should be avoided. Similarly, there should not be a window overlooking the manege or riding school. Any student will look out of the classroom window when there is something interesting to see, which again is clearly undesirable.

In Conclusion

Good classroom teaching depends on preparation and planning and the intelligent use of questions and training aids.

When students fall asleep in the classroom it is always the fault of the teacher!

Index

Figures in *italic* refer to photographs